self-care
Let's start the conversation

ROBERT ALLEN

Impactful Publishing, LLC
P.O. Box 11055 - Murfreesboro, TN 37129

Copyright ©2021 by Robert W. Allen (RWAllenBooks). All rights reserved.

ISBN – 978-1-7342606-5-6

All Scripture quotations, unless otherwise indicated are taken from the ESV: Study Bible: English standard version Wheaton, Ill: Crossway Bibles, © Copyright 2007. All rights reserved worldwide.

Cover Design: James McCarroll
Interior Design: Soumi Goswami, soumi.goswami.pub@gmail.com
Editor: Kate Rose and Wellington Johnson
Illustrations: Valarie Woods

Printed in the United States of America

66 Days to Unlearn & Change a Habit

SPECIAL THANKS

To James McCarroll for not only being family but also an accountability partner and brother. I thank you for your guidance, support, and constant sharpening.

To Tom H., Hadiza H., Rita N., Clarence M., Paul T., and Renee B., for taking the time to read this book and offer forewords and reviews.

Also, to my family who has supported me, been part of my learning process, my growth and instrumental in my becoming the man I am today. Your love and support have been a blessing.

The First Publication of the Restore &
Replenish Brand

This work is dedicated to all who wrestle with stress,
work-life balance, and the challenges of life.
May this book serve as a valuable resource
in your journey of self-care.

In the Memory of Deacon Wyatt Jones Jr.

Foreword

The experiencing of the following pages is akin to being invited by a skilled carpenter into his well-stocked workshop. The journey begins with *wondering*, in which the carpenter engages us about that which is to be crafted and shares insights about the task ahead. We are then welcomed into the workshop. We are introduced to tools and told stories about how others have used those tools to accomplish what they desired. The goal here is not to teach proficiency on every tool. Rather, we become acquainted with the range of what may be needed so that we can discern what specific tools we might pick up to use.

This skilled carpenter knows who will be doing the work. This carpenter knows that to shape the life we envision is, mostly, an inside job. And so, throughout the text, our guide poses questions and invites reflection. We are asked to discover our own inner knowledge, to draw upon our own inner wisdom. We are invited into a deeper exploration that might occur as we test out various tools and experiment with possible solutions. Our work is personal, and it need not be done alone.

In choosing the title, the author has been characteristically straight forward. He seeks to invite us into a conversation – at first one with him, then most importantly, one within ourselves. He shares of his own experience in order to activate our curiosity. He knows that healing is possible, and balance is within reach.

All we need do is start the conversation.

Rev. Tom Harshman, BCC,
Clinical Pastoral Educator

Self-care is vital to the realization of a better and more fulfilling life if we are able to navigate the complex matrix of human existence. Although many forces discourage tending to one's physical, spiritual, and emotional well-being, it should not be neglected. The discipline of self-care will redirect negative thoughts and actions towards a pathway of transformation. Fears are conquered. Potential is realized.

Joy and happiness become lived experiences rather than unrealized dreams.

If you have opened this book, you have taken the first step in beginning the conversation. Robert Allen brings a new approach to self-care in this volume. Rooted in experience, leavened in hospital chaplaincy, and fortified with soulful reflection, Allen has cultivated a unique method that is both practical and spiritual. He seeks to guide the reader away from fear towards one's potential. As you read through these pages, you will discover that Allen himself has turned his self-care into a deep and abiding care for others, including you!

And so, it is time to begin the conversation and discover the possibilities...

Dr. Hadiza Hamza,
Internal Medicine

TABLE OF CONTENTS

Introduction xi

CHAPTER 1 - Stress 1

CHAPTER 2 - What's shaping you 9

CHAPTER 3 - How Certain Positions Affect Us 20

CHAPTER 4 - How Does Your Job Shape Your Identity? .. 24

CHAPTER 5 - Mental Health Statistics 42

CHAPTER 6 - Coping Skills 47

CHAPTER 7 - Habits 55

CHAPTER 8 - Coping Skills and Self-Care............. 63

CHAPTER 9 - Self-Care Vulnerability................. 67

CHAPTER 10 - Physical Self-care......................72

CHAPTER 11 - Mental Self-Care 79

CHAPTER 12 - Emotional Self-Care................... 85

CHAPTER 13 - Spiritual Self-care 92

CHAPTER 14 - Mentors and Accountability Partners... 98

CHAPTER 15 - Filling my cup 115

CHAPTER 16 - The Four R's 129

CHAPTER 17 - Self-care Purpose......................142

CHAPTER 18 - Additional Barriers to Self-Care....... 146

CHAPTER 19 - Resilience and Sustainability..........149

Concluding Thought 158

Reference List 160

INTRODUCTION

What is this book about?

Self-care is not just a vacation or a spa day, it is a lifelong process. A process of knowing your own story and how it informs you. A major part of self-care is awareness and being mindful of what the "whole you" needs at that given time. Self-care should mainly be a preventive practice of caring for oneself, more so than a response to chaos.

As we age or circumstances in our lives change, we must be open and willing to adapt and apply different self-care techniques and tools that are the most beneficial and appropriate for that space and time in our lives.

Self-Care: *Let's Start the Conversation* is a book that looks to engage you, the reader, through personal stories and self-reflection. This book aims to be accessible to all people no matter their age, career path, faith, or leadership position. This book is ideal for people who have experienced and may still experience an imbalance in the work/home life, professional burnout, and/or leadership woes. In order to maximize the potential for learning and reflection, this book encourages you to take an introspective look at your life and be honest about areas that you need to improve. For this reason, it is important to read each chapter and spend time working through the issues that come to the surface during designed moments of reflection in the book, namely, the Reflective Pause. The Reflective Pause is made up of a series of questions that encourage you to delve into your own story and reflect upon your issues.

The hope is that through this book you can connect with your story as you enjoy the journey of becoming a healthier version of yourself. This journey is likely to involve tuning in to yourself, embracing intentionality, and ultimately being more mindful and aware. These changes can lead to a better understanding of what self-care looks like for you. As you read this book, you will see how each chapter builds on the next and creates a process. By the time you get to the final chapter of this book, you should not only have thought deeply about your life, but you will have also learned valuable lessons about some of your decisions, dispelled certain myths that once informed your choices, and put together a number of helpful tools to help you on your new journey of self-care.

Now let's start the conversation!

What is self-care?

Understanding self-care is a daunting task. The concept, introduced in the mid – 1800's, was initially a medical designation that indicated a patient who is able to take care of him/herself after a period of illness. Over time, the term self-care has evolved and has recently found a home among those in the clergy and is used to describe being able to care for one's needs to avoid professional burnout.

Burnout is a term that is prevalent in mainstream society. According to *Psychology Today*, burnout is defined as a state of emotional, mental, and often physical exhaustion brought on by prolonged or repeated stress. Though burnout is most often caused by problems at work, it can also be the result of personal stressors, such as parenting, caretaking, or romantic relationships.

On a personal level, I was always told to be careful of burnout, especially in professions like counseling and ministry.

What no one tells you is what to do once you have identified burnout. For many, the idea of self-care became almost cliché once burnout was identified. The idea of "taking a break," going on vacation, or even making big life changes became the de facto definition of self-care. The idea of self-care was misunderstood and often misapplied.

Self-care is so much more than a break, bubble bath, spa day, or vacation. Even among clergy, healthcare, and mental health professionals, many individuals hold a generic understanding of self-care. Due to over-usage and generic association, the term self-care has lost significant value. Some have even attempted to move past the idea of "self-care" altogether and utilize different terminologies such asW self-compassion and self-love, to name a few.

The goal of this project is to reintroduce and redefine self-care in a way that helps people reconnect with its true meaning. This said, I have defined self-care as employing what is needed to effectively fill one's cup in its most needful space. The goal is to redefine the way in which one understands and participates in self-care acts.

CHAPTER 1

STRESS

If you are anything like the rest of the population, you probably have had days, weeks, months, and maybe even years where you have been stressed.

You may also experience stress which arises from your relationships, work, or school environment. Your life could be so demanding that it becomes all work with seemingly little play. The privilege and responsibility of spending time with loved ones and family members sometimes often means leaving little time for yourself; if you are a single parent, or have a family, often you may feel the stress or pressure of being all things at all times. If you are single, you may have the stress of ripping and running, which I equate to the stresses that come with an active social life.

The responsibility of splitting time between the various areas of your life may prove difficult and sometimes exhausting. At first glance, you may say that sounds depressing. I must say when I began writing this section, I felt exhausted after I reread it! Yet, the purpose of this book is to highlight areas that may be potential blind spots which prevent us from taking the time to see things clearly.

These stressful and sometimes painful areas are what I like to call "stress pockets." Stress in itself seems very common, and we have all heard of it, but we are often taught that stress- "is just a part of life," and it is something we have to deal with.

This book is not a stress management book; there are many of those out there. However, this chapter is to help you identify areas of your life where you may find a need to place greater emphasis on your physical, mental, emotional, and spiritual wellbeing.

Stress, as defined by the A.D.A.M. (Animated Dissection of Anatomy for Medicine) medical encyclopedia, is a feeling of emotional or physical tension that can come from any event or thought that makes one feel frustrated, angry, or nervous. The U.S. National Library of Medicine notes three different types of stresses[1]:

- Routine stress related to the pressure of work, family, and other daily responsibilities.
- Stress that is brought about by a sudden negative change, such as losing a job, divorce, or illness.
- Traumatic stress, which happens when you are in danger of being seriously hurt or killed. Examples include a major accident, war, assault, or a natural disaster. This type of stress can cause *post-traumatic stress disorder* [P.T.S.D.].

For statistical purposes, according to the American Psychological Association, chronic stress is linked to the six leading causes of death: heart disease, cancer, lung ailments, accidents, cirrhosis of the liver, and suicides.

More than 75 to 90 percent of doctor's office visits are for stress-related ailments and complaints. Furthermore, chronic stress has been linked directly to affecting the brain, causing strokes, heart attacks, blood sugar imbalances, raised blood pressure, and ultimately reduced immunity and ability to heal. Some physical signs of stress include:

- Low energy
- Headaches

- Upset stomachs including diarrhea, constipation, and nausea
- Aches, pains, and tense muscles
- Chest pain and rapid heartbeat
- Insomnia
- Frequent colds and infections
- Loss of sexual desire and/or ability

The C.D.C. (Centers for Disease Control and Prevention) reports that 110 million people die every year as a direct result of stress. If this is true, it supposes that every two seconds, seven people die due to stress-related ailments.

Now let's not rush past these very important statistics. This is very significant. Take a moment and really allow this to sink in. Prolonged exposure to stress can prevent your body from healing. One hundred and ten million stress related deaths a year is a significant amount of people. I highlight these statistics not to scare you, but so you can have a better understanding of how stress can affect you and can possibly advance underlying conditions.

Stress is indeed a normal part of life. We all experience stress from our environment, our bodies, and our thoughts. Some stressors will be constant, while other stressors could be short term or possibly even a onetime stressor. Additionally, many of the positive changes in our lives, such as the birth of a new baby, a career change, a promotion, and a wedding, can cause stress.

If stress is an everyday part of life, what is the solution? If I had that answer, I would probably golf every day and live on a very big yacht. I do not have a fool-proof answer on how to eliminate stress, but I do have a recipe for helping you better understand yourself and what stresses you, so you may lessen the impact it has on your life.

There is a lot of materials you can find on ways of reducing stress, but I would like to address some long-term solutions that we do not generally think about. Usually, when we think about stress, we think about what is stressing us now; we think about work, family, school, health and finances.

Yet, we very rarely think about the whole body of work as it pertains to stress. What do I mean by "whole body of work"? These are stressors that we have endured since birth.

Have you ever been grouchy or in an indifferent mood for seemingly no reason? At times is it hard to shut off your brain, and just be present? Generally, when we experience moments of despair, indifference, inadequacies or simply being overwhelmed, these feelings can make it hard to enjoy even the simplest things in life. Stress can be a massive fun-wrecker and mood changer. For this reason, it is important to know yourself.

When it comes to stress, part of the general issue is being able to identify what our stressors may be. Some stressors are easy to identify such as trying to meet deadlines for a project or rushing to make it to an event on time. While other stressors, which we think of as a lessor stressor such as normal everyday routine stressors, we pay less attention to them. One of the reasons we pay less attention to the routine stressors is because we have become use to them. Mentally we unknowingly classify these stressors as insignificant. However, as I have discussed previously, stress when not managed can have severe consequences. So, in order to really understand the effects of stress and how to manage the stress, we first have to dig deep to identify all of our stressors and how they inform our behavior. Some of you may have heard of a term called *root cause*.

A *Root Cause* is an underlying or fundamental reason for something occurring. Said in another way, the root cause is the origin of something, and not the effect or symptom. Over the years, root cause analysis [R.C.A.] tools have been developed in various industries, including engineering, healthcare, business, and production, to help identify root cause issues.

R.C.A. is used on existing problems, prevention and helps to limit recurrences. For example, look at Japanese inventor Sakichi Toyoda, who introduced a concept known as the 5 Whys [diagram brought to you by Kanbanize] **"The basis of**

Toyota's scientific approach is to ask why five times when we find a problem... By repeating why five times, the nature of the problem as well as its solution becomes clear. "Taiichi Ohno"

Now let's take this same concept from a quality standpoint and employ it in a way that allows us to have a better understanding of ourselves by simply asking ourselves the "Why's". Through using this evaluation, we may better understand why we have triggers and stressors which cause us to display certain behaviors and reactions.

In the next chapter and as the book progresses, you will learn the value of re-engaging your story from a different perspective and asking yourself "Why".

Your story is important to know, as it informs your narrative. I believe what informs the way we have practiced self-care stems a great deal from what coping skills and habits we have developed over time.

Reflective Pause

During this time, I ask that you take time to intentionally identify stressors in your life. Take the time to think back as far as you can and list each stressor. What stressors are current? Ask yourself which stressor has which effect on you? How have you managed your stress?

CHAPTER 2

What's shaping you

I have found through the years that before you can jump into self-care, you must first take a reflective look at yourself. You have to know your own story. We often believe if we can get away from the problem, the problem will be solved. But we know that is not true.

For example, if a person is not feeling good; example: they have a pain in their side. Some people would take medicines to relieve their symptoms; but if the pain persists or worsens, the person might seek medical attention. Once at the doctor's, there will be tests to try to pinpoint the cause of the pain. After getting the results, the doctor would be better able to diagnose the problem. The goal is to treat the root of the issue. The same is true with self-care; it is a process of getting down to the genesis of what makes you tick.

I find that very often, we get caught up in masking pain, pretending the issues do not exist, or refusing to address problems and situations due to the amount of work it would take. On the other hand, I know that in certain situations, a person may be unable to afford having those issues addressed. In short, you get used to the pain and due to life's demands, you feel as if you do not have time or permission to address the pain or situation. Hence, you just keep going. I have been in a space where I have done just that. I just kept going and experienced many of the previously symptoms of stress such as low energy, insomnia, and even panic attacks.

However, everything we experience in life is a key component to what we need to help give us balance. Let's not forget the social, economic, and cultural aspects that play a factor as well.

Economically

Some people who are well off face challenges as well as those who are less fortunate. For instance, doctors are paid well. However, what people do not realize is that doctors also incur a massive amount of debt due to student loans. On the other hand, people who are financially less fortunate may believe money will solve all of their issues. They may feel that if they can somehow get out of poverty that everything would be great. Conversely, a middle-class person or small business owner may believe if they just close the next deal or get that once in a lifetime opportunity or position, that it will make everything better. These are the things we tell ourselves. These are things I have told myself.

For example, I don't consider myself a gambling man because I hate to lose. Not too long ago, however, the National Lottery's Powerball Pay-out was up to $300 million, and I decided to call one of my family members to purchase a ticket for me. I told my family member that if I won, I would split the proceeds with him.

While I waited a day or two for the next drawing, I had started to divide the money. I made a list. My breakdown looked something like this:

- $300 million minus the government cut left me with $150 million.
- My promise to split the money left me with $75 million.
- Minus my tithe of $15 million, which would be 10 percent of the $150 million, left me with $60 million.
- I planned to give $5 million to charities and foundations.

- I planned to open a $5 million trust account for each of my five children.

- I intended to give a total of $5 million to various family and friends.

- I wanted to set $10 million aside for investments.

- I wanted to use $5 million for business ventures.

- Finally, I wanted to use $500,000 on personal things such as clearing debt and enjoying a few of the finer things in life.

After all of that, I would still have a few million dollars leftover. As you can see, I had it all planned out. I said to myself, "Lord, you can bless this, can't you? I think this represents a good steward." Well, as you can guess, I did not hit the lottery, so back to work I went. But the mental exercise prompted me to do a little research on lottery winners. I have heard statistics in the past but never looked into it myself.

What I found shocked me. Research shows that lottery winners are more likely to declare bankruptcy within three to five years of winning the lottery.[2] Another article showcased 21 stories revealing how lottery winners were affected by their windfall. Some winners committed suicide, many marriages ended in divorce, several were imprisoned, and two lottery winners were poisoned.[3]

As good as I believe I am with money and boundaries, after conducting my research, I now have a different perspective.

What I noticed is many of these lottery winners had everyday issues. In fact, several I researched were already millionaires or well off before winning the lottery.

So, why these horror stories? It is simple: Money doesn't solve all problems. People are people, with their own set of challenges. Money can indeed relieve financial burdens, but if people don't change their way of thinking or begin to heal in their broken spaces, money will only help fund their dysfunction on a greater scale.

Reflective Pause

Has socio-economic status ever played a part in your stress? How has it informed your decision making? How has your economics help shape who you are as a person? How, if at all, has it defined you? What are some of the challenges you either face currently or have sacrificed in order to maintain a certain status? What were the effects?

Socially

Socially, there can be a great deal of stress that informs how we respond to people and what we carry. I am a believer that we are a sum total of all of our experiences. Whatever experiences we have either been exposed to or not exposed to have somehow shaped who and what we have become. Take for instance, a person who was raised in a very loving and affectionate family, that person will typically take on the characteristics of being a loving and affectionate person. Now there is an exception to every rule. I'm not saying all people who are raised in this environment will be affectionate. However, my point is whatever people are accustomed to, they typically gravitate to or the opposite, they repel.

For example, I was raised in a very affectionate family. My mother is the type of person who goes out of her way to help others. It seems as if she had fed, clothed, and housed various family members and friends for my entire childhood. While we didn't "come from money", however, what we didn't have in money we made up for in love and spending time with family.

While I had fun in my early childhood, things began to change once my dad became very ill. I was five or six at the time. While my mother was working to make up for the lapse, my dad's condition worsened. I was seven or eight when he eventually died. When he died, it didn't hit me until years later. I guess at that time, I really didn't understand grief. However, after his death, my brother, sister, and mother all dealt with his death differently. Before his death, my sister joined the Army, but neither my brother, who is named after my father, nor my mother coped well.

After my father's death, the biggest thing I remember was having to move. For me, this meant moving away from my school and all my friends. My dad's death, my sister's leaving and getting married, and my moving away from my school and friends were all concrete memories for me. These events were each an enormous loss. The first move would be one of more than four. I attended a total of four different elementary schools. While my mother was trying to cope with my father's death, I experienced another grief: loss of a parent and loss of a community.

As I grew, I associated myself with various people, some good and some I should have steered clear from. But I missed my father, I missed my community, and often I just wanted to be accepted, to have stability, and to fit in. Even as an adult, I have always felt most comfortable when I can experience time with my family and friends.

From childhood to becoming an adult, there are both positive and negative social influences we will be exposed to from parents, family, classmates, friends, and people we interact with on a daily basis. Social influences can be great, but they also can be problematic. Today is much different from when I was younger, now we have to include the influences of social media as well.

Brokenness comes in many shapes and sizes. Being broken not only affects you, but in many cases, it has the capacity to affect the people around you. How does that relate to self-care, you ask? Again, if we are to really understand self-care, we must begin to take a more holistic look at ourselves. Including the good, the bad, and the indifferent. A closer look at ourselves will help us identify how to better care for ourselves. Many of us have gone through life masking issues, after issues, after issues, and putting band-aids on wounds, instead of taking the time to heal those wounds.

Let's take another story from my life. Many of my friends would say that I am competitive. I believe I am, for the most part. One day I remember my competitiveness got the best of me and it ended up making me feel like a jerk. On a bright sunny day at home, I was playing a game with my daughter. We were talking trash back and forth, and I scored on her multiple times. Part-way through the game, tears began to develop in her eyes, and she said, "Dad, I love playing games, but what is the point of being competitive if you're not having fun anymore?" I was stunned. At that moment, winning meant more to me than spending quality time with my daughter.

Now, if I am honest with myself, my competitiveness comes from feeling excluded when I was younger. Some of my earliest memories of playing board games with my cousins are not really good memories. My cousins were older than me, and when we would play Monopoly, they would team up to get me out first so they could continue the game. I would leave the game mad and in tears because they were not fair.

The same kind of thing happened in basketball and other activities. Also, it does not help that I came from a very competitive family to begin with. My uncle was a gamer of chess, checkers, various card games, etc., and boy, was he a hard teacher. When he taught anyone how to play a game, there was no room for error. He was a 'yelling in your face' kind of teacher. Nothing was "just a game" with him; he did not like losing.

However, these experiences helped shape and mold who I became. After the experience with my daughter, I became more aware of my competitive nature. I am still competitive, but her words ring in my ears every time I participate in a game. I cannot let competitiveness take the fun out of the game. Remember, stress can become a fun-wrecker.

Reflective Pause

After reading this section, what speaks to you most? What from your childhood carries over to your here and now? Again, think of what things have help shaped who you are. Who and what have been major social influences in your life? What were some of the negative influences? What were the positive influences? Have you ever been in a space where you just wanted to fit in or be accepted? At what length did you go to be accepted or to be part of something?

What sacrifices did you make? How have these experiences shaped who you are and impacted your decision making?

Culturally

Culture also has a significant role in how it influences people. Culture can vary on a very large scale. Culture is affected by state, city, neighbourhood, family, and friends; it can even include religion, to name a few.

The definition of culture can consist of anything from behavioral patterns, arts, ethics, literature, and beliefs of particular societies. It can be said that culture is a part of our lives from the day we are born, even if this isn't something that crosses our minds on a daily basis. However, once mentioned, we can truly start to see how culture affects us and our lives, for example, how living in a certain culture affects the way you are brought up.

The environment we are brought up in, and live in, has a significant impact on the way we communicate, act and behave within society. The way we were raised also affects our behavior as well as influencing our personal traits and habits that are displayed as we grow older. The way that your parents educated and reared you has a massive influence on the way you act today. Therefore, everything that you learn in your life, whether significant or small, is influenced by the way we see the world, through culture, when we are infants. For example, if your parents are kind and loving, it is likely that you will become kind and loving as well. In other words, it is likely that we progress toward being who we are within our cultural environments.

Of course, there are some intra-cultural beliefs that are not universal, such as attitudes towards marriage. Marriage, as well as attitudes to dating and courtship, widely differ throughout different cultures; however, you might find that emotions don't vary significantly between cultures.

Many cultures in the world today are highly influenced by political, social, and economic systems as well as religious belief systems, which is why some cultures may seem as though they are unchangeable and strictly traditional. However, the social aspect of culture has become ultra-progressive. Think of how influential social media has become in the lives of so many today. Yes, social media, has its own distinct culture. In the year of 2020, various movements such as *Black Lives Matter* and *All Lives Matter* have created a distinct culture as well.

Reflective Pause

Consider your culture. what beliefs, attitudes and behaviors have you adopted from your culture? What role have various cultures played in your life? Do you fit in, in your culture?

CHAPTER 3

How Certain Positions Affect Us

The Family Man or Woman

I am the biological father of three children but, in total, a father of five. I have a 19-year-old daughter, an 18-year-old son, a 17-year-old son, a 13-year-old daughter, and wait for it—a 1-year-old son. I know, I know, pray for me! While my last son was not planned, he is a beautiful gift from God. Without bringing all my baggage to the party, being a husband and father can be exhausting. I find myself going from one sporting event to the next. Often, I feel like an uber driver that has to pay to drive. When my daughter was younger, it was gymnastics, then soccer, coupled along with my son playing golf, coaching his little league team, as well as baseball and soccer. Most weekdays were dedicated to practices, while the weekends were devoted to games.

Does this sound familiar? Go to work, pick up the kids, go to trial, get back home, cook dinner, help the kids with their homework, get everyone ready for sleep, clean the kitchen, sit down, maybe get a T.V. show in with the wife, and before you know it, it is time to go to sleep to wake up to do it all over again. Sounds normal, right? As a parent, you can't wait for the sports and activities to begin to slow down. In some way, you sort of get a little of your life back. However, you still seem just as busy, but now you are trying to fit in spending time with friends and family. Making up for lost smooches with the spouse or praying that one of the grandparents or friends would say, "Hey, let us take the kids for the weekend!"

But what happens if you live somewhere new and don't have the support of grandparents or friends? When I moved from the Midwest to the Western part of the States, I didn't have a ready-made support group. Over time, a support group was developed. I recall working two jobs, being a full-time dad, in ministry. When my children were smaller, I worked a full-time job, ran my own business, preached several times a week, coached football, and was in a graduate program. I will say I am a master at time management. I found ways to incorporate my children into coaching and ministry. I always ensured my family got the time it needed. I did my best to be present.

However, I recall one interaction with my very active daughter, who was about three or four years old at the time. I believe it was a Saturday. I had just worked an overnight shift, coached a football game, came home to do yard work, and came into the house and plopped down on the couch.

My wife had to run errands, and my daughter was running 200 miles per hour and just filled with energy. She also wanted to watch a movie. I popped popcorn, made us a fort in the living room, and ensured she had everything she wanted. My eyes started to drift slowly, and my daughter being who she is, opened my eyelids with her fingers and said, "Dad, you have to watch the movie too!" She held my eyelids open until I finally sat up straight and watched that movie.

That experience is now something I often think about and chuckle. For one, my daughter is hilarious. She wanted daddy time, and holding my eyelids open with her fingers was her way of making sure she helped her daddy stay awake. That memory warms my heart every time every time I think about it. However, when I look at it through the lens of self-care, I cannot attest that I was truly present. I was operating from a place of exhaustion. Everyone and everything else were getting my attention.

Everyone was getting time, and not necessarily quality time, but what about me? Where was my time to truly decompress? Where was my time to exhale? I made time for family vacations, which were friendly getaways, but boy, were they exhausting. I recall going to Disney World for a family vacation. All I wanted to do was sleep. But sleeping was not an option. Disney World was expensive, so we did everything we could from the park's opening to its closing. But where was my self-care?

Reflective Pause

Engage this section. Family and friends are essential to life. However, the same people we love are often the very same people who requires most of our attention. Do you or have you ever struggled with the stressors or demands of work life balance? Do you wrestle with spending quality time with those you love? When you spend time with family and friends, how much time do you leave for yourself? Do you wrestle with exhaustion or worry?

CHAPTER 4

How Does Your Job Shape Your Identity?

These days, our identity is associated with our work. An article in the Chicago Tribune[4] ("Just can't escape the daily grind" by Charles McNulty, February 21, 2016) argues that even today's movies are all about our jobs. Spotlight, this year's winner of the Oscar for best picture, it is a prominent example of this trend. McNulty puts it this way:

Taken collectively, the somber message of these movies...is that we have become our jobs. "I think, therefore I am" has been updated to "I work; therefore, I exist."

Technology has made employees accessible around the clock. Workplace settings are increasingly open and they encourage community, which is great, but this might also mean a narrowing of the worker's life to fellow workers. Money and status are seen as the marks of success, so we work harder, smarter, and longer.

Retail/Sales

With the rise of stress in the workplace, companies are trying to do more and more to offer incentives. In the late 90s, I worked as an intern for a rent-a-car company.

I learned the ropes quickly. I was on my way and was being groomed for management. You would be surprised how much money a branch manager makes at a rent-a-car company. If you were at a busy branch, you could earn six figures quickly. If you were an area manager overseeing several departments, you were making ideal money.

I knew two area managers who were making over $200,000 a year quickly. The company I worked for used to rent out a billiards hall every month for its employees. It was well needed especially after working 50-60 hours a week as a branch manager or even as a regular worker.

The company often rented out places for staff members to blow off steam, but if you had a family, you needed to get home after working all of those hours. If you didn't have a family, you found your way to the parties but soon realized you had to be to work the next day.

Social life was made for your days off in this industry. The money was terrific, but you had to hustle for it. Again, where was the self-care? At this age, self-care was a foreign language.

Education Experience

If you know anything about teaching, it is fun, exciting, and exhausting. Teachers perhaps spend more time with students in a day than the students do with their parents. Being a teacher means pouring your time and effort into every student. At times, a teacher serves as a pseudo-parent. They have the sole responsibility of managing class behavior while teaching and multitasking to meet every student's needs. Additionally, as students have diverse learning styles, often a teacher has to go over several different ways of breaking down a subject to ensure all students are grasping the information. As a teacher, I often held tutoring during lunch hours and after school.

I taught in both private and public schools in the inner city of Detroit, Michigan. In both school systems, I devoted time to each student. I had students who would come to me after school or in between classes to discuss personal issues that were taking place in their homes.

I have had students whom I had to teach the principles of good hygiene. There were times I would get to school early and open up the locker room for a student to have hot water. I would bring in hygiene supplies and made sure they had what they needed to start the day. Pouring into the lives of my students was a calling for me, but it was exhausting.

Furthermore, what happens with teachers who have their own families? This may be even more exhausting as they have been around children all day, and now they are at the point of being around their own.

I have many friends who work in the education system, from early childhood education to the collegiate level. Many educators bring their work home, and not just papers to grade.

Even those who work in the capacity of being an administrator, social worker, lunch aide, and facilities worker bring home the mental and emotional stressors of those they educate and serve.

Coaching

Playing sports and coaching sports are impressive; however, my time as a coach was fun and fulfilling, yet exhausting. Whether you are coaching little league, high school, or on the collegiate level, you have been tasked with training someone. As a minor league coach, you are continually pouring into youths and teaching them the game's fundamentals.

At times you would go to practice early to help those who need a little more attention. Often, minor league through high school coaching means that the coach works a full-time job and usually has a family. Coaches are often taken for granted. They pour into children, sometimes much like teachers, and can often take on a pseudo-parent position as they ensure that the player's general needs are being met on and off the field. As a coach, you try to create a family atmosphere, instilling principles such as teamwork, hard work, dedication, conditioning, preparation, work ethic, and trust.

Coaches are often ridiculed for one thing or another. You have parents to satisfy, and you have players to invest in and manage; and let's be honest, in all of this, you want to win as well. If you have a few losing seasons, it is almost as if all the good you were doing on and off the field does not matter. Being a coach, where coaching is an additional responsibility outside of the regular 9 to 5, usually takes away from your family time.

Some people get to coach their children, but if you have more than one child, those children who are not in sports will time taken away from them.

As a former high school football coach, I know the stresses of ensuring your players meet the mandates as a student-athlete, with acceptable grades and proper behavior in class. Also, the pressures of providing support to ensure they were taking care of their responsibilities at home and being the right person on and off the field. Seriously, it is like having between 30 and 50 additional sons you are looking after, especially if you are the head coach. I had the opportunity of coaching with some fantastic coaches. Coaches who invested a remarkable amount of time away from their families to coach sports. I remember having to pick players up, take them home, prepare food, or have food for less fortunate players.

I know what football has done for me as a coach, and for many players. Sports, in general, serves as an outlet for them as well. So, giving back in this capacity was a no-brainer; I loved everything about the game. Throughout my coaching experiences, I have had several players become not just players, but more like family. I had players that I would pick up to go to church with me. Players with whom I would sit and help with their homework. Some players had family situations and even had to live with me at one time or another. All of these instances mean an increase in responsibilities, which means that you are expending extra time and energy pouring into more people.

I have never regretted any of the teams I have coached. I believe those experiences were a blessing; particularly the relationships that have come out of coaching. However, I hold coaching up as another area and field of work where people have to take time out for self-care. Time away from pouring into others, so that they may be poured into.

Healthcare Field

Being a board-certified chaplain has been one of the most rewarding and yet, most taxing career callings of my life. As a contributing member of an interdisciplinary team with doctors, nurses, social workers, respiratory therapists, and paramedics, to name a few, I have been part of some of the most difficult yet also the most rewarding experiences of my life.

As I have stated previously, sometimes we take for granted other professionals and what they do and how their career can have lasting emotional effects on them. Often doctors, be they surgeons, internal medicine doctors, and even primary care physicians, can carry the emotional weight of ill and dying patients.

Hospital Staff and Healthcare Field

As a chaplain, I served primarily as the emergency room chaplain. On one occasion, a day before the holidays while working in a level 1 trauma center, I relieved the overnight chaplain. When I arrived for a shift, I got a call to meet the chaplain in the emergency room. After arriving at the emergency department, the overnight chaplain explained that there was a 5-year-old girl who was brought in 15 minutes before she began to experience complications. The chaplain then introduced me to the patient's mother sitting in a quiet room (a room within the waiting room). I introduced myself as the chaplain and one of the healthcare team members that would be caring for her daughter. The mother gave me a little history regarding the patient, including that she was born with specific medical issues, but that she had been doing well. I asked if any other family members would be coming down to support her. She explained that she has two other children who were being watched by the family and called the patient's father to inform him. I explained that I would be back and forth between checking on the patient and checking with her, giving any updates that I had been asked to provide by the medical team.

When I went to the emergency room, there were many people, more than I had seen at any other time in an emergency room. There were upwards of 15 people in the room. There was the trauma team, the pediatric team and the cardiac team, and everyone was working hard on reviving this 5-year-old girl. The patient would decline, and then the rally.

A few minutes later, the patient would decline again. I was back and forth between the patient and her mother, simply stating to the mother that the team is working and had a specialist on board to assist. The pediatric and specialist team had a relationship with the family. Several doctors from peds to the specialty team had all come out to talk to the mother at some point, just to gather more information.

After over an hour of trying, each team had near exhausted every option; when one group was tired, another team jumped right in, trying whatever they could to stabilize and save this young girl's life. No one in the room was willing to give up. They would not, they could not give up; everyone was determined that this little girl would not die.

After more time had elapsed, I advised the doctor in charge, "I believe it is time." Then I asked, "Are we doing more harm than good to the patient at this point?" I recall the look on the doctor's face. The look of failure, defeat, anguish, pain, and most of all, hurt. I explained it was now time to talk to the patient's mother as every attempt each of the teams had tried was unsuccessful.

The doctor looked at the time and was very emotional as he struggled to pronounce the time of death. When I walked in with two of the physicians, the lead doctor, and head intern, the mother saw the look in our eyes and knew.

That day, I heard a sound I had never heard in all my life; it was the most gut-wrenching whelps of hurt and pain of which I cannot begin to describe. The mother fell to her knees with her arms stretched out and laid prostrate on the floor. Nothing other than these loud whelps could be heard through the walls of the waiting room.

The doctor broke down, the resident broke down, and tears streamed down my face as I kneeled to hold the mother up. After some time, I asked the mother if she wanted to go and be with her daughter.

As we made our way to the E.R. room where the 5-year-old girl laid lifeless, each of the teams from the specialist, nurses, imaging, EKG, unit clerks, and everyone in between, were all in tears.

As the mother approached her little girl, the room began to clear out. The mother thanked everyone for their efforts. I recall, when she made it to the patient's bedside, one of her pigtails was sticking straight up. Her mother said, "There you go again, that one little pigtail that I can't get right." She proceeded to take down the one little pigtail and begun to re-braid it. That was my breaking point. I had to excuse myself for a few minutes to release some of my emotions.

See, at the time, my daughter was the same age as the patient. Many of the people in the room had small children or grandchildren around the patient's age. After some time, additional family members arrived, including the child's father, and each time a new family member came, a new wave of grief began. For the rest of the day, I ministered to the family and the staff.

This was probably one of the most emotionally taxing days of my life as I went to check on every team member (more than 20), who each required time to grieve.

Others do not see the stress, strain, emotional attachments, and baggage that professionals endure from the outside looking in. Again, we say it is their job, but they are human too. They have emotions and feelings, as well. For everyone involved, the family and the staff, this holiday felt slightly different that year, and I know for me, this holiday remains somewhat saddened.

I was happy to be there that day, to offer myself to the family and the staff. With this, I was emotionally drained. Most people in the healthcare field try not to take situations like that home to their families. They often hold their feelings in and categorize them, but as we know, that is not a healthy way to cope. Now think of all the other healthcare fields, from home care and hospice to cancer centers, neonatal units, cardiac centers, and paramedics who live with these stories more often than they would like. The question is: Have they allowed someone to help them process and deal with their emotions? Some do, some can't, and others don't know how to address the emotions or even know when it is time to get help until it is too late.

Military/Law Enforcement/Fire

Military personnel and first responders are also recognized as critical roles. I had the esteemed pleasure to serve my country as a sergeant in the United States Army. I was also fortunate to serve my community in law enforcement and fire as well.

Let's take a look at military life. I have served with some of the bravest men and women in the United States Military. I also come from a military and law enforcement family and have many friends who serve as firefighters. No matter if it's a military, law enforcement, or fire department shift change, or assignment, the primary final words of the commander are, "Be safe, watch your six (meaning your back) and make sure you come home."

While this could potentially be the most extensive section in this book, I will not elaborate too much, as it should be a book of its own. For this segment, I would like to discuss how everyone who goes out does not always come back. Many who serve in these fields have witnessed tragedy and trauma, and those who stay in these fields until retirement often have lost someone close to them or someone they know. Most times, these fantastic careers come with a cost not only to those on the job but also to their families.

When a soldier goes off to deployment, they leave behind the family. My sister was part of Desert Storm, and my niece was just 3 months old when my sister's unit in Germany was being activated.

My niece was sent to us in the U.S. while my sister served in the military in Germany. Like three of my cousins who served in this war, many people were separated from their families. A soldier's sense of duty to country and their responsibility to family often creates conflict and strain.

Making accommodations to ensure that your family is taken care of can be taxing. Also, some soldiers who come back do not always come back mentally intact. Many times, people fail to see the effects on the soldier and their family. This is also true of police officers and firefighters. These are some of our first responders who run toward conflict and danger for the safety and protection of others. Coming from a law enforcement family, I have witnessed first-hand the traumatic effects that losing one of their own can have on a police officer.

First responders are faced with some of the following: the danger of routine traffic stops gone wrong; firefighters running into buildings and not everyone on the team making it out alive. Do we consider the strain and pressure of the group or partners and their families? Recently, tensions between civilians and police have grown, and it appears that we have reached times where distrust between the community and law enforcement has increased and become complicated. It is stressful to have brothers and sisters who wear the uniform while also having brothers and sisters who don't wear the uniform in conflict with one another. If one police officer makes a mistake, given enough media coverage, it casts a shadow on all who wear the uniform. Coming home with life, sound mind and body, along with the job's task, could indeed be very heavy. Yet how does the soldier, police officer, firefighter, and other first responders care for themselves?

Leadership/Management/Business Owner

One role often left out of self-care is leadership. No matter if you are in the military, government, for-profit or non-profit, Fortune 500, or small business, everyone in administration faces challenges. If you have ever served in a professional leadership position, I am sure you have heard "to whom much is given, much is required." I have had the opportunity to serve in various leadership roles, including manager, director, and CEO. No matter the position of leadership, they all come with complexities. Many don't understand the stress and struggle of leadership. I find it remarkable that many people desire the status and luxury of being a boss, owner, or leader, yet when given the responsibilities, many don't make it. I have seen leaders in high-level positions burnout quickly. It seems as if turnover in various leadership roles is on the higher end. Let's look at a few statistics regarding hospital executives from 2013.

Hospital Executive

- The average hospital CEO tenure is under 3.5 years

- Fifty-six percent of CEO turnovers are involuntary
- When a new CEO is hired, almost half of CFOs, COOs, and CIOs are fired within nine months
- Within two months of a new CEO appointment, 87% of CMOs are replaced [5]

A more recent study conducted by the American College of Healthcare Executives explains this further. That study states that comparing the record high of 20 percent of CEO turnover in 2013, the last five years represent the most extended period during which turnover has remained elevated to this level since the study began in the early 1980's. [6]

Clergy

I have had the opportunity to work as a board-certified chaplain, a ministry leader, associate pastor, and interim pastor. I have seen some wonderful and amazing things happen while serving in ministry. However, the work of a minister (of any denomination or religion) is not all roses. The call to a church can be very taxing. For those who work in the area of ministry, stress and fatigue are two elements you endure. No matter if you are starting a church from the ground level or taking leadership of a thriving church, the stressors of the calling can be both rewarding and exhausting. Note, the term *clergy* is a very generic term. Thus, I am using this term to incorporate many labors in the ministry field to include chaplaincy, traditional pastoring, evangelism, and being a missionary, just to name a few.

In one statistical study regarding ministry, I pulled a few statistics that pointed out the following.

- 90% of the pastors' report working between 55 to 75 hours per week
- 80% believe pastoral ministry has negatively affected their families. Many pastor's children do not attend church now because of what the church has done to their parents
- 95% of pastors do not regularly pray with their spouses
- 33% state that being in the ministry is an outright hazard to their family
- 75% report a significant stress-related crisis at least once in their ministry
- 90% feel they are inadequately trained to cope with the ministry demands
- 80% of pastors and 84% of their spouses feel unqualified and discouraged in their respective roles
- 90% of pastors said the ministry was completely different than what they thought it would be like before they entered the ministry

- 50% feel unable to meet the demands of the job
- 70% of pastors always fight depression
- 70% say they have a lower self-image now than when they first started
- 70% do not have someone they consider a close friend
- 40% report serious conflict with a parishioner at least once a month
- 50% of pastors feel so discouraged that they would leave the ministry if they could
- 50% of the ministers starting will not last five years
- 75% report severe stress causing anguish, worry, bewilderment, anger, depression, fear, and alienation
- One out of every ten ministers will retire as a minister in some form
- 94% of clergy families feel the pressures of the pastor's ministry.
- 80% of spouses feel the pastor is overworked
- 80% of spouses feel left out and underappreciated by church members
- 80% of pastors' spouses wish their spouse would choose a different profession
- 66% of church members expect a minister and family to live at a higher moral standard than themselves [7]

Reflective Pause

This was a lengthy section; however, take some of the examples I shared with you, and now consider your career. What stressors are associated with your career? How do you cope from day to day with these stressors? What challenges do you face on a daily basis?

CHAPTER 5

MENTAL HEALTH STATISTICS

A study conducted by Richard J. Krejcir explains a significant increase in hypertension, obesity, cardiovascular problems, and depression associated with those who work/labor in ministry. No matter if you are a manager of a restaurant, clothing store, hospital, or anything in between, the world and workforce are becoming more competitive; burnout, stress, and mental illness are on the rise. Again, speaking of mental illness, let's be transparent and talk about what is not most common or popular to say, the rise of anxiety and depression. If you didn't know, anxiety disorders are the most common mental illness in the U.S., affecting 40 million adults in the United States aged 18 and older, or 18.1 percent of the population every year. While anxiety disorders are highly treatable, only 36.9 percent of those suffering receive treatment.

According to the Anxiety and Depression Association of America, anxiety disorders develop from a complex set of risk factors, including genetics, brain chemistry, personality, and life events.[8] While we can do little to address the genetics side, we can focus on the life events portion. Again, if you remember in the first chapter, think root cause.

Let's take a look at the chart below. While we can discuss an array of stressors, I want to focus for a second on two very common mental health areas, anxiety and depression.

Generalized Anxiety Disorder (GAD)	GAD affects 6.8 million adults, or 3.1% of the U.S. population, yet only 43.2% are receiving treatment. Women are twice as likely to be affected as men. GAD often co-occurs with major depression.
Panic Disorder (PD)	PD affects 6 million adults, or 2.7% of the U.S. population. Women are twice as likely to be affected as men.

Social Anxiety Disorder	SAD affects 15 million adults, or 6.8% of the U.S. population. SAD is equally common among men and women and typically begins around age 13. According to a 2007 ADAA survey, **36% of people with social anxiety disorder report experiencing symptoms for 10 or more years before seeking help**
Posttraumatic Stress Disorder (PTSD)	PTSD affects 7.7 million adults, or 3.5% of the U.S. population. Women are more likely to be affected than men. Rape is the most likely trigger of PTSD: 65% of men and 45.9% of women who are raped will develop the disorder. **Childhood** sexual abuse is a strong predictor of a lifetime likelihood for developing PTSD.
Specific Phobias	Specific phobias affect 19 million adults, or 8.7% of the U.S. population. Women are twice as likely to be affected as men. **Symptoms typically begin in childhood**; the average age-of-onset is 7 years old. Obsessive-compulsive disorder (OCD) and posttraumatic stress disorder (PTSD) are closely related.

Obsessive-Compulsive Disorder (OCD)	OCD affects 2.2 million adults, or 1.0% of the U.S. population. OCD is equally common among men and women. The average age of onset is 19, with 25 percent of cases occurring by age 14. **One-third of affected adults first experienced symptoms in childhood.**
Major Depressive Disorder	The leading cause of disability in the U.S. for ages 15 to 44.3. MDD affects more than 16.1 million American adults, or about 6.7% of the U.S. population age 18 and older in a given year.
Persistent depressive disorder, or PDD	This is a form of depression that usually continues for at least two years. It affects approximately 1.5 percent of the U.S. population age 18 and older in a given year (about 3.3 million American adults). Only 61.7% of adults with MDD are receiving treatment. The average age of onset is 31 years old.

As you can see, I have formatted several areas in bold that highlight disorders that begin in childhood. According to the CDC (Center for Disease Control), in the U.S., 7.1

percent of children aged 3-17 years (approximately 4.4 million) have diagnosed anxiety. Also, 3.2 percent of children aged 3-17 years (approximately 1.9 million) have been diagnosed with depression.⁹ Hopefully, by now, I have painted a good enough picture or made a good case regarding stressors and the need and importance of self-care.

Reflective Pause

How has your mental health been impacted with all that you do? Do you go days without feeling like yourself? Do you find less enjoyment in things that once brought you happiness? Do you seem to be more frustrated or easily agitated?

CHAPTER 6

COPING SKILLS

Now that we have discussed stress in some detail, we will now shift to how we cope or manage these stressors. Again, life is full of stressful situations that we cannot control. What we can control, however, is our response to those situations. It might feel impossible, but this is where coping skills play an important role in our mental health. By improving our tools for coping with stress, we can take a step back from our immediate reaction and give ourselves space to find a better approach. For example, you're frustrated by a situation at work. The immediate reaction might be to quit or send a slew of angry emails. This might feel good in the moment, but it won't help you in the long run. You could be left thinking, "Why did I just do that?" after the dust settles. Instead, a coping skill will soothe or distract you from the frustration, and then you can act from a place of intent rather than instinct.

Unhealthy Coping Skills

When negative thoughts or feelings are overwhelming, or we are stuck in rumination mode and those thoughts and feelings don't go away, we naturally develop coping strategies. People don't want to feel badly for very long and we're experts at finding ways to numb or avoid these negative feelings. Research shows that people with childhood trauma are more likely to rely on unhealthy coping skills. Some examples of unhealthy coping skills include drinking alcohol, using drugs, unregulated eating (too much, too little, or bad quality), and spending too much money. Those are not effective coping skills because they don't actually make us feel better. Alcohol, for example, is a depressant and you will wake up feeling worse after attempting to drink your problems away. It can also cause substance dependence. In general, healthy coping skills will lead us to clarity, while unhealthy coping skills lead to bigger problems. If you have a tendency to use unhealthy strategies, it can be helpful to work with a therapist to identify your triggers and replace the unhealthy activities with more beneficial choices. [10]

The Two Types of Healthy Coping Skills

According to the Centre for Studies on Human Stress, healthy coping skills are either problem-focused or emotion-focused.

Problem-focused coping skills

With problem-focused activities, a person looks for practical ways to reduce or solve the issue that is causing the stress. In a work-related situation, for example, you might talk to your manager directly, establish boundaries for time management, or apply for another position. People who like to write to-do lists and check off items might prefer problem-focused coping skills. With that style of coping, it's important to remember that baby steps are okay. You need to balance positive momentum with self-compassion. You cannot solve everything right now, but you can find a few things that can greatly improve your stressful situation. The good news is that you're not numbing or avoiding the problem and leaving it to fester. Some issues have very clear solutions and anything we can do to move toward our goal will help lower our stress.

Emotion-focused coping skills

Emotion-focused coping skills help you to manage feelings caused by the situation rather than the event itself. There might not be a problem to solve, or it's a singular occurrence that can't be avoided. In this case, you need to soothe or balance your emotions with the right activities for you.

This could be exercising, petting a dog, taking a bath, spending time in nature, or watching a movie. Sometimes we just don't want to handle a situation quite yet and we need more downtime. An emotion-focused coping skill helps to nurture and repair, recharging for the next step.

To make sure that you're nurturing and not numbing your emotion, make sure that you can name the feeling. If you're not sure what you are feeling, try consulting a feeling wheel. This style of coping isn't intended to chase away the emotion — instead, sit with it for a while. Be nice to the feeling. Don't judge yourself for having the feeling. Have faith that, in time, the feeling will pass. Mindfulness-based meditations can be a great way to process emotion-based stress.

Negative and Positive Coping Skills

Coping skills are the activities in which you engage in order to cope with a stressful lifestyle or times when you find your emotions difficult. However, there are also coping styles. Coping styles deal with the ways that people personally prefer to deal with their stress. They are the umbrella that coping skills come under. If you are able to determine your coping styles, it will be much easier to find out what your coping skills are likely to be. Therefore, you can more easily find the coping skills that you will benefit from the most.

Knowing what your coping styles are can help prevent negative patterns of dealing with your stress. Just as there are coping styles that will create positive results in helping alleviate your stress or difficult emotions, there are negative coping styles. Understanding which coping styles work for you can help you to identify which are positive and which are negative, therefore helping you to break bad patterns in your life and allow you to deal with your stress more effectively.

Personally, I think it is easier to replace the negative coping styles with positive ones, rather than just attempting to eliminate the negative behavior. When you try to stop something negative in your life, it could leave you feeling empty, often feeling as though there is a void. Therefore, it leaves a stressor behind that might be what caused you to begin using the negative coping style in the first place. If you see replacing the negative behavior with a positive one as something you need to do to be able to cope with stress more easily, you will find yourself more motivated to replace this negative behavior. If you feel yourself becoming anxious or stressed, ask yourself what you can do that will positively help the stressful feeling, rather than using a negative coping skill. When you understand which of your coping skills are negative, it is easier to prevent yourself from engaging in those behaviors in the future. As soon as you find something positive with which to replace the negative coping skill, it will become a lot easier to eliminate the negative altogether.

Negative Coping Styles

Denial: Denial is pretending the problem does not exist in the first place. It is usually maintained by excessive alcohol use or overworking, so you can continue pretending the problem is not there.

Self-blame: Blaming yourself for your problems, issues, or difficult situations leads to depression and the feeling of being in a negative rut. It is much harder to come out of your negativity if you are consistently blaming yourself for the problem.

Venting: This is an external way of dealing with your issues. Sometimes it can be healthy to share your problems, however, continuing to constantly bring up your negative problems will not help solve them and may lead to strained friendships over a long period of time. Venting is important; however, venting can lead into trying to get people to feel sorry for you, or perhaps trying to get people to be on your side to affirm you.

Surrender: Surrendering, as it pertains to negative coping styles, is giving in to the negativity and feeling sorry for yourself, as well as continuing to repeat those negative behaviors. Again, people who enter the surrender stage may find it very difficult to reach normalcy again.

Avoidance: Avoidance is a way to pretend the issue or situation is not there, or alternatively blocking the problem out. A symptom of avoidance can be seen in people who are both socially and emotionally withdrawn.

Overcompensation: This is overcompensating for the problem. For example, if a person feels sad that they have a problem, they may act out through aggression to counter the problem.

Positive coping styles

Humor: pointing out the funny side of your problem or situation.

Seeking support: asking for help from family members or friends can help ease the intensity of emotions when dealing with problems. Like they say, a problem halved is a problem solved! We will speak more about this in the section regarding mentors and accountability partners.

Problem-solving: locating the source of the problem can help in finding solutions. If you know what the root cause of the issue is, it becomes much easier to find ways to alleviate the stress and focus on long-term solutions.

Relaxation: practicing calming techniques, such as meditation, can really help with managing your stress and giving yourself a time-out to find calm, away from your issues or situation.

Physical recreation: Exercise can be a great way of finding time away from your problems. As it is known, exercising releases endorphins which are chemicals produced by the body to alleviate stress and pain. Finding the time to go on a walk or do some yoga could really help ease your stress.

Adjusting expectations: Adjusting your expectations can help to prepare for stress that may be coming up. Whether you are moving to a new house or changing jobs, adjusting your expectations of yourself can help to stop the pressure you may be feeling.

Now that you have a few examples of positive and negative coping skills, begin to work on replacing some of your negative skills with some positive ones. As much as possible, we must begin to limit not only the negative inner voice chatter, but replace it with something positive, which leads to better stress management and a better version of yourself!

Reflective Pause

Can you easily identify your coping skills? What coping skills have you used that were positive? What coping skills have you used that were negative? How have your coping skills been either beneficial or not beneficial to your overall self-care?

CHAPTER 7

HABITS

How exactly do you think you form your habits? Do they even affect you? Can you believe something as simple as having a cup of coffee every morning can be a dreadful habit? I had not paid much attention to some of the simple but harmful habits I formed in my life until recently!

Throughout our lives, we pick up or form habits, some good and some bad. However, we have to take note that these habits are crucial elements that direct our lives. Let's look at the definition:

Habit

1: a settled tendency or usual manner of behavior.

2: an acquired mode of behavior that has become nearly or completely involuntary.

3: a behavior pattern acquired by frequent repetition or physiologic exposure that shows itself in regularity or increased facility of performance."

Now, if we begin to just think about this for a minute. I began to look up quotes regarding habits and came across a few that spoke to me. The first says.

"Forty percent of your actions are not conscious decisions, but habits" – Charles Duhigg

In Charles Duhigg's book, *The Power of Habit: Why we do What we do in Life and Business*, he lists very interesting facts about habits. He explains,

- Our life is, to a large extent, the sum of all our habits – good or bad.
- We can take control of our life by changing our habits.
- It is hard to shake off a habit since it takes an average of 66 days before a new habit takes root in our brain.
- Habits never truly disappear. They are just overpowered by other habits.

- A survey showed that the daily habit of self-acceptance was the cause of most people's happiness.

- Cravings are the brain's motivator. For something to become a habit, our brain must crave it.[12]

Duhigg also explains how habits form. In his estimation, he explains habits are the collection of behaviors that could be as simple as having coffee every morning or as complicated as running away from problems when they come.

He also explains that these habits did not happen overnight and that we adopted them little by little over time into our lives and psyche until they became second nature. I would have to agree. As I take a step back and look over many of the things that I have gotten involved in over the years, I can say 'this rings true.' For instance, when I think about the emotional part of losing so many family members, my coping mechanism became a habit. Many of the times I engaged in coitus, it was like I was absent in mind. I was there, but I really wasn't. For many of my family members, their habit was revealed in another form of addiction, such as the use of alcohol.

In the 1990s, a group of researchers from the Massachusetts Institute of Technology discovered a neurological process that is at the core of every habit, what Duhigg would coin as the simple 3-step loop and suggested it is extremely powerful and that it is hard-wired into the brain. The loop contains three central elements.

1. **Cue** – is any trigger that tells your brain when and which habit to use.
2. **Routine** – is an activity, emotion, or behavior.
3. **Reward** – is how your brain determines if a loop is beneficial to you or not.[13]

This makes perfect sense. If a person is anxious, which is the *cue*, they could smoke a cigarette, which is the *routine*, and the *reward* would be feeling less anxious. I know, for my mother, cigarettes and coffee were her vice. When her doctor told her that she needed to stop smoking, after 40-50 years of doing so, it was tough. To change her behavior, she began to eat peppermints or hard candy. However, when the doctor told her she couldn't drink coffee, oh, boy! Now cigarettes are linked to lung cancer amongst other things such as C.O.P.D., etc., but coffee?

Let's look at it another way. Some people eat when they feel hurt or depressed, which means overeating or what you are eating could cause health concerns. The point is, as the definition of the word habit pointed out, a behavior pattern acquired by frequent repetition or physiologic exposure that shows itself in regularity or increased facility of performance was actually manifesting in my mother's life.

As I really began to ponder the importance of habits, it led me to the second quote, which reads:

"You'll never change your life until you change something you do daily. The secret of your success is found in your daily routine" - John Maxwell.[14]

John Maxwell is a renowned author that is highly regarded for his motivational books. As I read this quote, I began to think about my day-to-day routine. Again, you may be asking yourself when you will get to the part about self-care. Well, we are getting there.

What I have noticed in the two quotes is that I have to pay more attention and become more aware of what has become routine to me. In doing so, I have found both some positive and negative routines. One positive is that I like going to the gym. I love it. I am at the gym at least four to five days a week.

It helps me to let out aggression. In high school, I played football, when that ended, I joined the Army, and when that ended, I took up mixed martial arts, and with work and all the other responsibilities I had at the time, there was not much time for the forms of exercise which I had become accustomed to.

I see that in every space where something ended, I had to fill that space with something else. After a while, what I figured out was that healthy outlets became different ways of masking my hurt and pain.

When I accepted my call into the ministry, my old coping mechanism of being promiscuous to deal with hurt, pain, or frustration was no longer an option. I used work, ministry, and my children as scapegoats so that I didn't have to deal with the reality of not taking a football scholarship. I became a workaholic and a success-a-holic, nearly killing myself in the process.

At one point, I was working two jobs, preaching several times a week, coaching football, making time for my family, running my own business, martial arts, and attending graduate school for my second master's degree.

Exhausting is what it was. I was truly shortening my life expectancy and didn't even realize it—some of the things I did to alleviate pain, were cultural. As an African American male, it was always ingrained that I had to work harder than everyone else, be more aggressive and competitive. For me, I didn't want to grow up poor, not like when I was little. I wanted to make it. I wanted my kids to have all the things I couldn't have and experience all the things I couldn't, so much so that when I think back, trying to accomplish it all, I can't remember enjoying 90 percent of it.

The very thing I was trying to prevent, seeing my mother work hard to ensure we had, the struggle she endured, I was now enduring. I wasn't struggling financially the same way she did, but I was repeating the same behaviors.

I recall one gut-wrenching moment, one that I would never forget, and it still brings me great anguish. I remember going to Kentucky Fried Chicken with my mother. My uncle and his family were there, and we approached the counter to place our order. My uncle and his family all ordered, and my mother and I got to the register and my mother didn't have a lot of money. I remember she ordered the smallest thing they had so that I could eat. I'm not sure to this day why we just didn't order with my uncle, because my mom had taken care of him time after time. Anyway, my mother and I shared three chicken wings that night. There was a look I saw on my mother's face, and I read it as one of hurt. Could it have been that she expected more from my uncle since she periodically took care of him? Could it have been she felt excluded? Could it have been her pride of not having enough money? I remember saying I wasn't that hungry, even though I was, so that my mom didn't feel what I assumed to be angry and hurt. All I know was that day I saw, experienced, and felt an emotion that I did not like, and more than that, I felt like I couldn't talk to anyone about it. Remember, most in my family didn't talk about emotions, so neither did I. But this was a formative experience that contributed to my obsession of not wanting to be poor and not struggling.

Reflective Pause

After reading this section, what have you learned about your habits? What are your true takeaways? Can you identify any habits that you've used both past and present? Which are good, which are bad? Which habits have changed over time? How have your habits informed your behaviors? What are your thoughts on the two quotes? Don't shortchange this section, really take a deep dive and be honest with yourself.

CHAPTER 8

COPING SKILLS AND SELF-CARE

Hopefully, you are still with me and engaging in each section. Let's talk about coping skills now. Hopefully, through my story, you have seen thus far some of the things that drove me. Not that I did anything wrong, and most certainly not because I did anything right. I was just doing my best to survive in the narrative I created for myself based on my exposure and experiences.

As you can see by now, I had many feelings, but not necessarily a lot of healthy releases. In several previous chapters, I shared how I coped with my emotions. Hopefully, in this section, you will understand how coping skills are helpful and can adversely interfere with one's self-care.

In the therapeutic arena, we teach a great deal about coping skills. While there are various definitions regarding coping skills, I will focus on this particular definition that suggests, "coping skills are tools and techniques one can use to help them handle difficult emotions, decrease stress, and establish or maintain a sense of internal order." [15] Let's say, for example, a person becomes angry. That person's coping skill designed to keep them from lashing out may be to take three seconds before responding. Another coping skill may consist of doing push-ups to calm yourself down before re-engaging in a tense conversation.

While I believe positive coping, skills are needed to address an immediate reaction, this is not all there is to self-care. If we are conducting proper self-care, the aim is more in addressing the root and underlying issue so that one does not have to solely rely on a plethora of various coping skills.

Try doing push-ups for at least three seconds or whatever positive coping methods works best for you. However, consider this: if a person with anger issues decides to address the root cause of their anger, this can decrease how often they lash out. Therefore, the person does not have to rely solely on a coping skill.

Let's look at it from a different perspective. Let's take a child who has asthma. When they get worked up and become too active too fast, they risk having an asthma attack.

A parent will often tell the child to slow down, and the child takes a few puffs of an emergency inhaler. The inhaler has now become an emergency response to the activation of the child's asthma. The inhaler's purpose is to give the child immediate relief and prevent them from having a full-blown asthma attack. So, in this example, I liken the inhaler to a coping mechanism.

Now when I think of self-care in this analogy, I see self-care as the parent teaching the child to be more aware of what causes the symptoms once the child develops an understanding and becomes more in tune with what their body can and can't do. The awareness in knowing when to push and when not to push themselves makes the need and reliance on the inhaler less frequent.

In my personal experience and over the years, I have been involved in the practice of helping others. I have found that many people (myself included) rely more on coping skills and less on self-care. For me, my coping skills became a mask.

If I were overworked, upset, frustrated, or exhausted, I would typically do the same activities to cope with presenting feelings or emotions. Most of the time, what I found was, like the inhaler, my coping activities became emergency responses that eventually became less and less effective in dealing with the symptoms.

I became drained faster and looked to these emergency responses more frequently instead of learning how to confront, deal with, or manage the source of the issue beforehand.

Reflective Pause

Have you supplemented coping mechanisms as self-care? Have your coping mechanisms been masked? If so, in what way?

CHAPTER 9

SELF-CARE
VULNERABILITY

I have hosted and conducted training in the area of self-care. When I teach on the topic, I always explain that one of the primary elements needed to begin self-care starts with a person's willingness and ability to be vulnerable. Being vulnerable means being uncomfortable, and let's face it, most people don't want to be uncomfortable. You may ask, "Why is vulnerability a major component?"

Well, let's look at it this way. A person has to admit there is a problem, issue, challenge, or concern in order to address it. Most people get hung up, once they have identified the problem, as they do not know how to handle the question, issue, or concern.

This can be seen in some of the previous chapter's data, which displayed how many people suffer with or battle anxiety, yet the diagnosis goes untreated. In my work in the fields of counseling, law enforcement, military, coaching, and ministry, I have worked with or know individuals who have burned the wick at each end of the candle until they exhaust themselves.

I have personally burned out and have stressed myself out on more occasions than I would like to admit. As previously mentioned, when I discussed my CPE experience, it was not until that course that I became aware of how deep my unwillingness was to deal with myself and my needs.

So much so that the mask of being successful, being a good husband and father, and continually working to better myself professionally overtook my need to become a healthier person. No matter what you achieve professionally or gain materially; it all comes with a cost. We must determine if the ends justify the means. Let me put it another way, is what we are sacrificing worth the energy we are dispensing to achieve?

In life, we must make tough decisions; however, I advocate that we should make these tough decisions from healthier spaces as much as possible. Again, I will equate this with our ability to be vulnerable and honest with ourselves.

In my estimation, the second step to self-care would be identifying what we need. Self-care for one person may not be the same for another. People are at different stages of their lives.

We must realize that who we are is a total of our experiences, be it good, bad, or indifferent! How we choose to address or not address our challenges and experiences will dictate how we live our lives and how we relate with and to others. If we come from a toxic environment and don't address the toxicants, we will ultimately struggle with relationships. If we often suppress emotion, pain, and dysfunction, they will likely manifest in other ways and behaviors.

Think of a pressure cooker. At some point, the steam has to release. It will either slowly release steam via a pressure release valve or the pressure cooker itself will indeed explode. For those whose temperament doesn't give way to exploding, the example for you would be to isolate and wither away slowly from the inside out.

For instance, it is like an apple that appears shiny from the outside, but once you peel back the skin, one can see that it has slowly rotted from the inside over time. In our case, the rot could be indicative of hurt, pain, anguish, guilt, stress or being overwhelmed; you name it.

I have done a lot of research on self-care, and various writers and experts have divided self-care into either three, five, or six components. North Carolina State University has self-care divided into three significant parts, physical, mental/emotional, and spiritual. [16]

On many occasions, mental and emotional self-care are divided into their components. I have also seen self-care component variations to include physical, mental, emotional, spiritual, social, and practical. While I believe the initial three, physical, mental, and spiritual are core components, I see the value of speaking to all six members: physical, mental, emotional, spiritual, social, and practical.

Research from North Carolina State University explains that self-care is an active part of enhancing your health quality. Some people may think that nurturing the self is only for the fragile, weak-willed, or the slacker; in other words, they feel that it certainly couldn't be for the strong and ambitious.

Yet research supports, and I agree, that self-care is a vital part of maintaining good health and living a vibrant life. Simply put, self-care is not just an occasional manicure, "chilling out," or a six-pack.[17]

One very simplistic definition I have come across numerous times regarding self-care is as follows:

"Actions you perform to take care of your physical, emotional, and mental needs. Self-care is all about communicating with your soul and saying "Hey, what do you need right now?". Then doing it."- Unknown.

Reflective Pause

Please take a moment and think about how this picture speaks to you. What is the picture saying? How, if at all, does it relate to your life either currently or in the past?

Understand some things you simply do not need to carry. What have you been holding on to that you no longer need to carry? Are you willing to be vulnerable with yourself and are there feelings you have suppressed? If so, can you readily identify them?

CHAPTER 10

Physical Self-care

Physical self-care includes how we are fueling our bodies, including how much sleep we receive, what we are doing to remain active, and the basics of how well we are caring for our physical needs, which include but not limited to, sex and exercise. Physical self-care also includes those things we seemingly take for granted, such as attending appointments, taking medication as prescribed, and managing our overall health.

Some of the most common excuses why people neglect this form of self-care consist of:

- 'Busy' Lifestyles

- Believing you are already in good shape
- Guilt in taking the necessary time
- Motivation
- Costs

I can speak and have spoken volumes to a few of these excuses. Again, when you have school, a career, and family responsibilities, it is very easy to neglect your physical needs.

Doing a lot doesn't necessarily equate to proper physical self-care. I would justify what I was doing with statements like, "I just wish there were more hours in the day?" Chances are, even if there were more hours in the day, some of us probably wouldn't take the time to hit the gym or exercise. I would probably say it's an 80 percent chance that you would just do more work. I know making time to work out or even to eat healthily can be a challenge. I have friends and family who try every new diet that comes out. They last all but a few months, and it's back to the same old food choices. I remember having a conversation with my wife. She was trying some new diet where she was not eating carbs. She lost a few pounds after a few weeks and then was stagnant. I would always communicate the importance of exercise to her. She would reply, "With school and work I just don't have the time."

I explained, "It's funny how you can make time for shopping, running errands, etc., but you don't have time to work out or exercise." You know what happened, right? Yes, she gave me "the look". The look that says, "You better not say another word!" look. Do you know what I did? I said another word! What I was trying to convey to her was that dieting without exercise would not yield the results that she wanted. Like any good spouse or one who cares for another, I want the very best for her to achieve her health goals and be healthy. Over a semester, I saw her get more and more tired, cranky, and irritable.

I could do nothing less than to be emphatic toward my wife. When I am not doing something that keeps me active, I can get irritable and cranky also. A few years ago, I worked a full-time job in a leadership role and performed a significant contract for my own company while completing my third master's degree. I ensured I made time for my wife and family, went to the gym twice a week, and played in a competitive football league.

Running a spiritual care department, being an emergency room chaplain, in a leadership role at my church, and running my own consulting company was very taxing. The competitive football league, coupled with me going to the gym a few days a week, was a fantastic way to decompress while giving my body the physical exercise I needed. I felt like I was in great shape, almost as good I thought as I was in my 20s. However, one year ago, my wife and I received a pleasant surprise; she informed me she was pregnant!

When the baby arrived, I had the care of the baby after I got off work due to our work schedules. By the time I got off work, it was straight to the babysitter and back home, by then, my wife was leaving out the door to begin her workday.

Some changes took place. I was no longer able to go to the gym with a newborn at home. I couldn't play in the football league anymore and going to the gym would mean that I would have to wake up super early and go before work.

I tried that a few times, but let's face it, I know me, and I'm not such a good morning person. After several months, I lost my motivation to work out, even on my wife's off days, which were the opposite of mine. I lost the groove, and before I knew it, I became lethargic, moody, and boy, did I lack motivation. I could feel my energy levels being depleted, and I just felt yucky. Once the baby got a little older, and I purchased a pull-behind enclosed wagon for my bike. I used that a few times, but it just wasn't my thing. As a licensed therapist, I can honestly tell you I began to feel resentment and I began to see small signs of depression. I reached out to one of my mentors and explained the situation, and we problem-solved my options.

After a few weeks, we decided to increase our membership at our gym that offered childcare, yes it cost a little more, but that meant I could get back. I still couldn't play football, which was my passion, but I could join a few exercise classes that challenged me.

A good friend of mine left his gym and joined my gym, which led to a workout buddy. I thought I was in good shape with all the running around I was doing with work, but I needed a physical release in reality. I was at the point of losing my mind, and a good portion of the reason was caused by me not making the physical time I needed for myself.

Remember, we are all different, and our physical activities may not be the same. However, you must choose things that work for you. I know that following routines may get old and boring, and often, many people lose interest in doing the same old thing. So, I encourage you to switch it up.

You may want to take a few classes; cross fit, martial arts, kickboxing, cycling, or take the time to go on morning or afternoon runs. I would suggest you try an activity for 30 days and switch to another.

One of my very best friends says she is allergic to working out, and if you fall in this category, I will say pick physical things you can enjoy doing or at least try something that seems fun. If you used to play volleyball, swim, ran track, or participated in any sports, now is the time to give it a try. If time doesn't allow you to do those things, just find something that interests you.

Another helpful tip is to get one or a few workout buddies. Not just any workout buddy(s), but people who will hold you accountable for meeting up and working out.

The gym is not for everyone; heck, even at the gym, classes can get boring, so I take a course for a few weeks then try something different. I rotate things out and new stuff in, to keep me motivated and my interests up.

Reflective Pause

Think back, what in this section on physical self-care resonates with you? Can you ask yourself the hard questions such as: Are you getting enough sleep? Are you getting enough exercise? Are you doing your best to fuel your body well? What are some of the sacrifices that you have to make to ensure you can practice excellent and consistent physical self-care without the excuses of being too busy, believing you're already in good shape, feeling guilt in taking the necessary time, motivation, and costs? Write out a plan for the next 30 days, stick to it, and see if you realize any improvements.

Before we move on to the next chapter. Please take a look at the following picture. In what way does this picture speak to you? Does anything in particular catch your eye? If so, what?

Mind Full or Mindful?

Chapter 11

Mental Self-Care

I feel that we have touched on this subject in a few areas already, but I want you to keep in mind that there's a strong connection between our physical body and our mental wellbeing, which is our mind. Sometimes, when I am angry, I need space to be able to clear my mind. I like to have physical activities to bring me down if I am frustrated or upset about something.

When I am exhausted and stressed, I like to be in serene places in nature, be it near the water, in the mountains, or somewhere surrounded by trees and greenery. Our mental status is so important.

As I previously showed with statistics, mental illness is rapidly increasing. Depression, anxiety, strokes, heart attacks, stress attacks, and burnout is at an all-time high. Our brain sends messages to every part of our body; without it, we can't function. Yet, this is often one of our most self-abused organs. When we stress the brain, we are subsequently stressing other organs as well. We push and push and continue to push ourselves to the point of constant headaches and stress attacks. Early in my counseling career, I thought that going away on vacation was good mental self-care. I said to myself, "Oh I'll go on a trip just to get away from it all." I would go on vacation and still get phone calls, or by day three, I wanted to get back home because I knew the work was just piling up.

Have you ever gone away for a few days and return to hundreds of emails? Yes, me too. Isn't it depressing when you have to read them all and respond? I soon realized that going away did not necessarily fix the situation but offered a band-aid to what I needed.

While in seminary, one of my assignments was to read a book called *Boundaries* by Henry Cloud and John Townsend. If you don't have this book, I strongly recommend you not only read it but purchase it for your library.

The book's subtitle is: "When to Say Yes, How to Say No to Take Control of Your Life." The title in itself speaks volumes. The writers explain:

Having clear boundaries is essential to a healthy, balanced lifestyle. A limit is a personal property line that marks those things for which we are responsible. In other words, boundaries define who we are and who we are not. Limitations impact all areas of our lives: Physical limitations help us determine who may touch us and under what circumstances — Mental limitations give us the freedom to have our thoughts and opinions. [18]

For so long, a work ethic that was ingrained in me didn't necessarily equate to me practicing good mental self-care. When working in the ministry, counseling, chaplaincy, teaching, coaching, business, etc., people continuously pull on you to meet their needs. Coming from a family like mine, especially with my mother, who is probably one of the most giving and welcoming people I know, we were taught to help and give to others. At the high school I attended, one of its mottos is "Men for Others" and "Selfless Services." If you work in a demanding career and especially in a human service field, the demands can be high. There have been times that I had stretched myself so thin trying to meet others' needs that I blanked out. I mean, I went full-blown catatonic. I also began to have panic and stress attacks. I would be so depleted of energy giving to others that I had no energy left for myself. I was in total mental exhaustion.

Years later, an instructor gave us a story to read during a retreat, called the Raccoon's Lesson. I attempted to look up the story, but the author was unknown, the closest source

I found was from a Native American Legend, but the story was attributed to an unknown author even then. The report reads as follows:

The forest was full of homeless and wounded creatures after the great fire. The Raccoon Tribe ravaged all the nearby mountain cabins and brought food to the hungry. The Tribe of little bandits worked long and hard hours to supply what was needed to help the forest's other friends.

Mama Raccoon was busier than most of the others of her Tribe, mending the cuts and bandaging the burns of those who came for assistance. Days dragged into moons, and still, the needy came in hordes. Mama Raccoon was the protectress of the frail, the children, the injured, and the underdog. She took her mission very seriously and labored day after day with little relief or rest. The other raccoons became increasingly worried because Mama was close to collapsing.

One morning, Mama Raccoon fell over, barely alive. The others took her to the burrow and nursed her as best they could. In her lapses of dreams and consciousness, Mama Raccoon heard the Earth Mother saying, "You gave all of your strength to others, forgetting to weigh the consequences. The little bandit in you, who robbed food from those who had a lot, giving it to those who had none, has lost her balance. In order to heal, you will need to see the error of robbing yourself of all your energy and giving it away, leaving you with none."

Mama Raccoon learned these lessons and got well. Now she teaches these same lessons to humankind, reminding them to give to the best of their abilities without robbing themselves of their health or sense of wellbeing. [19]

As you can see, the moral of the story is: You have to take care of yourself! Having healthy boundaries that you abide by helps you in your quest for mental and physical stability. There are times we feel we have the capacity to keep pressing on; however, we should not stretch our largest and most vital organs to the brink.

Another part of practicing good mental self-care is taking breaks and doing your absolute best not to allow things to pile up before recognizing that you need a break. If my work in the medical field has taught me anything, it has taught me that it is my responsibility to care for myself. I must have a level of discipline consistent with what my body needs. I also remind myself to effectively rely on my accountability partners to care for myself, especially amid challenges. How much of life do we truly miss out on because we are preoccupied with other matters on our minds? Date night is a little less fun when the other person is present physically, but not mentally or emotionally. Participating in family or friend outings are less fun when we are preoccupied.

In my work, I contact people who struggle to be calm, silent, or just be present. If you fit this category, I genuinely suggest you re-read the section on the effects of stress and how it impacts you in the long run. Having an active life is not necessarily a negative thing, in that, we must be sure to leave space to rest our minds and bodies so that imbalance does not become the result of our lack of self-care. The inability to find this balance often comes from learned behavior. Many times, we need reminders to take care of ourselves. With joy and appreciation, receive reminders.

Reflective Pause

What in this section on mental self-care resonates with you? Can you name times that you have missed out on enjoying life and spending quality time with others because you were mentally preoccupied? Take a deep breath and be honest with yourself and name instances when you were present physically, but not mentally? Identify barriers that prevent you from being present or taking the necessary time to decompress? Write at least three solutions you can apply to alleviate those barriers.

CHAPTER 12

EMOTIONAL SELF-CARE

Emotional self-care is closely related to mental self-care. How we think, what we think, how we feel and how we see ourselves all relate to self-care. Chances are if we are drained emotionally, it affects us mentally and physically as well. When we think of depression, most people have a mental image of a person who is completely incapacitated or unable to function.

However, depression presents itself when "lesser" depressive symptoms are ignored. Emotional satisfaction can be difficult because it causes us to be vulnerable and being vulnerable can be scary. For this reason, when dealing with emotional vulnerability, I suggest we use wisdom. You may have an awesome friend who is a good listener, yet will they hold your conversation and your deepest thoughts in confidence?

Are the people you surround yourself with emotionally stable enough to offer you good advice?

Emotional self-care is one of the hardest areas to wrap our minds around, because emotions change from day to day. If you are in a relationship and going through a rough patch, stress on the job, loss of a family member, career change, moving from home or a variation of other life factors, each of these have the ability to contribute to the stressors which impact your emotional health.

Everything in our life can be going awesome, however, if we fail to address those little pockets of depressive characteristics, good can become bad very quickly. As we have seen on television, many stars have committed suicide, have undergone psychotic breakdowns, and/ or nervous breakdowns. From, a normal, non-star, perspective one can say, "How could they have been fighting depression, when they seemingly had it all?"

Again, one person's breaking point and stressors can be very different from another person's. For this reason, it is very important that we stop putting off the small things. 'Small things' left unresolved have the ability to create more disruption and dysfunction over time. The key here is to stop putting things off and moving so quickly to the next thing.

Let's look at relationships. No matter if you are married or unmarried, if you have spent a significant amount of time and emotional space with someone and for some reason there is a break in the relationship, moving on quickly doesn't necessarily equate to a happier life.

When someone dies, throwing yourself into more work may mask the pain, but it doesn't solve the issue of being hurt. In my experience as a therapist, most often, we do not allow ourselves adequate time to process and transition into our "new normal."

Let me be the first to say that I have not mastered this portion of self-care, but I have identified through experience and education, how to be more effective and successful in this area. For me it boils down to processing, transition time, mindfulness, and being intentional.

Mindfulness in essence means simply to be conscious or aware. In the therapeutic arena, mindfulness is a technique used by therapists to focus on one's awareness in the present moment, while calmly recognizing and accepting one's feelings, thoughts, and bodily sensations.

Mindfulness therapy has been used for years to effectively treat or reduce stress, anxiety, and depression. For the sake of self-care, we must begin to pay more attention to our emotional needs. From a personal standpoint, in much of the work I have done, I typically give a lot of myself to others.

I have suffered from depression, due to not having the proper tools, such as mindfulness, to address my emotional deficits. Wisdom and experience have taught me to offer greater credence to my emotional capacity. As a therapist, I must be cognizant of the energy I expend while serving others. I can only see so many patients before I have to take time to decompress and work on my emotional awareness and health.

Regarding my story, I have mentors that I communicate with. I have other therapists I speak with who work in difficult situations. I surrounded myself with people who can again offer good advice. I took the time to be serious and transparent with myself to say, "I can't be everything to everyone", and sometimes it takes being strong enough, and taking time for yourself without feeling guilt, to practice an art form. Which I thought of as "The Power of No." "No" gives you some freedom. "No" doesn't have to be final, it could also mean no, not now. However, "no" requires discipline and mindfulness. Knowing why you are saying "no" is important. In my case, a great deal of my emotional deficits came from my inability to say "no" or to say "no, not at this time." The "no" for me is because I have met my emotional capacity, or I have allowed my emotional state to suffer to the point of complete depletion.

After being aware or mindful, the next step is processing. When we go through any emotional break, exhaustion, or depletion, we need to have adequate time to process. Most often, this is the step that is left out or that we lack putting effort or focus into. When we are in work mode or "get it done" mode, we very rarely allow ourselves adequate time to process how we feel and why we feel the way we feel. In many instances, we go through life making not so great decisions because we are doing so out of a lack of emotional intelligence.

Think for a second, when we are emotionally depleted, we are apt to make decisions that we normally would not have made if we were our healthier self. Some people who suffer breakups rush into another relationship without allowing themselves adequate time to heal. However, what we fail to realize by doing so is that we bring whatever unhealed spaces of that relationship there are, into the next. Most of my counseling clients have stated that they rushed into another relationship, got married, and now they and their spouses are miserable.

When I dig deeper, a few themes seem to be consistent. In these instances, what seems common are individuals rushing into relationships to fill voids or they bring baggage from how they were raised into their current relationship. Please understand, we are the sum total of what we have experienced or been exposed to. This being the case, unpacking these experiences are very important.

If we step outside of the relationship realm, we can move into the professional realm where processing is still relevant. For instance, a manager has to terminate several employees. This manager could have possibly built a great relationship with these employees. After having the conversation with each staff member and explaining that their position has been eliminated could be very exhausting and tough for the leader.

Yet, as a leader, the manager is expected to go on with work as usual. Let's pause for a second. We often look at this from the point of view of the employee that lost the job, which is necessary. Yet, what about the manager? What about the manager's emotional capacity? Afterall, managers are human as well. Who is available for this person to decompress and heal emotionally?

Often in the corporate sector, this crucial step of processing is overlooked. Hence, what usually takes place is a manager who eventually becomes burnt out and this begins to spill over in many other facets of the manager's life. This can include isolating, engaging in unhealthy coping methods, and even depression.

Reflective Pause

What in this section on emotional self-care resonates with you? Name times you have made unhealthy decisions due to being emotionally depleted. List areas of unhealed spaces that have affected your emotional state. Have you healed from them? If not, are you willing to address these issues so you can live a happier and healthier emotional life?[1]

CHAPTER 13

SPIRITUAL SELF-CARE

Spiritual self-care, no matter the practice, suggests that quiet time alone with your God, creator, or energy is important. I will be speaking mostly from an Abrahamic faith standpoint for this particular section.

As I have mentioned previously, the body is made up of mind, body, and spirit. Those who may not believe in a higher power may not subscribe to this, yet for those who do, this section may be quite beneficial. Within Christianity (Bible), Judaism (Torah), and Islamic (Qu'ran) faiths writings, all are consistent in encouraging the person/believer to spend time with God.

One's spiritual beliefs can play an important role as to how the work of faith can bring strength and give direction. Understanding how one's faith influences their life's walk will differ from person to person.

As for me, my faith assists me with my humility. From a Christocentric standpoint, my faith promotes self-care. In teaching segments on self-care, there are multiple scriptures that inform me to stop, pause, and remember that I cannot do it all.

Let's take a look at the following scriptures:

- Matthew 14:23 - After He had sent the crowds away, He went up on the mountain by Himself to pray; and when it was evening, He was there alone.

- Luke 5:15-16 - But the news about Him was spreading even farther, and large crowds were gathering to hear Him and to be healed of their sicknesses. But Jesus Himself would often slip away to the wilderness and pray.

- Mark 1:35 - In the early morning, while it was still dark, Jesus got up, left the house, and went away to a secluded place, and was praying there.

- Mark 6:31 - And He said to them, "Come away by yourselves to a secluded place and rest a while." (For there were many people coming and going, and they did not even have time to eat.)

- Mark 6:45-46 - Immediately Jesus made His disciples get into the boat and go ahead of Him to the other side to Bethsaida, while He Himself was sending the crowd away. After bidding them farewell, He left for the mountain to pray.

Without getting too deep, what I found in the scriptures was Jesus taking time for himself to be in solitude. Luke 5:16 explains that Jesus often withdrew to places of solitude.

When teaching this particular segment in the faith-based sector, I often ask people, especially the workaholics, if resting, prayer and strengthening one's faith was good enough for Jesus? This is clearly a rhetorical question because He left us an example, but are we following?

When facilitating trainings, I often receive the "deer-in-headlights" gaze, which means people look at me puzzled as they are processing what I just said. After processing, people typically begin to think about how they need to take time for themselves.

One really good scripture for leaders is found in Exodus 18:13-26.

The next day Moses sat to judge the people, and the people stood around Moses from morning till evening. When Moses' father-in-law saw all that he was doing for the people, he said, "What is this that you are doing for the people?

Why do you sit alone, and all the people stand around you from morning till evening?" [20]

And Moses said to his father-in-law, "Because the people come to me to inquire of God; [21] when they have a dispute, they come to me and I decide between one person and another, and I make them know the statutes of God and his laws." [22] *Moses' father-in-law said to him, "What you are doing is not good.* [23] *You and the people with you will certainly wear yourselves out, for the thing is too heavy for you. You are not able to do it alone.* [24] Now obey my voice; I will give you advice, and God be with you! You shall represent the people before God and bring their cases to God, [25] and you shall warn them about the statutes and the laws and make them know the way in which they must walk and what they must do. [26] Moreover, look for able men from all the people, men who fear God, who are trustworthy and hate a bribe, and place such men over the people as chiefs of thousands, of hundreds, of fifties, and of tens. [27] And let them judge the people at all times. Every great matter they shall bring to you, but any small matter they shall decide themselves. So, it will be easier for you, and they will bear the burden with you. [28] If you do this, God will direct you, you will be able to endure, and all these people also will go to their place in peace."[29] So Moses listened to the voice of his father-in-law and did all that he had said. [30] Moses chose able men out of all Israel and made them heads over the people, chiefs of thousands, of hundreds, of fifties, and of tens. [31] And they judged the people at all times. Any hard case they brought to Moses, but any small matter they decided themselves.

When I read these scriptures, verses 17 and 18 leaped right off the page, as they spoke to my core. Moses' father-in-law confronted him and explained that taking on such a heavy task was not good for him and that it was too much of a burden for just one person. I recall numerous occasions when I have overwhelmed myself, often doing so in the name of and for the sake of ministry. I have often not taken the advice of those who came before me, and have suffered because of lack of wisdom, discernment, and just being plain hardheaded. Within these key verses it was instrumental, that although Moses was the leader, he listened to the wisdom of his father-in-law.

Moses, like so many of us, was so focused on the task that he failed to see that he had the help he needed with him the entire time. Part of being a leader is not doing it all on your own but building others to aid you in the task at hand. In context, what Moses truly needed was sacred time and space in order to be the leader God needed him to be and to have the energy needed to invest in the people who would help him lead.

More times than I would like to admit, I have allowed myself to become spiritually depleted by not taking the necessary time for myself. My unwillingness to leave tasks unfinished has taken a toll on me in various ways.

Henry Cloud said, *Spiritual boundaries help us to distinguish God's will from our own and give us renewed awe for our Creator. Often, Christians focus so much on being loving and unselfish that they forget their own limits and limitations.*" [32] For this reason, we have to be mindful to create sacred space and time to engage God in our faith. Some examples could consist of being intentional in setting time aside as Jesus did to retreat from the crowds and busyness of life, to find a quiet space to truly commune with God and exercise our faith.

Reflective Pause

What areas of this section speak to you? How does your faith inform or influence your life and the decisions you make? Transparently speaking, are you as engaged in your faith as you wish to be? What are some ways you activate your faith? In what areas do you take on more than you should? Do you use faith as a scapegoat to add more onto your plate?

CHAPTER 14

MENTORS AND ACCOUNTABILITY PARTNERS

In Chapter 8, I spoke briefly on the importance of mentors and accountability partners. Here I will explain more in depth concerning the importance of having both mentors and accountability partners. A person who would later become my mentor hosted a meeting, and while in this meeting, they explained the difference between a coach and mentor. While this was a professional setting, he expressed that a coach offers techniques and tips on helping a person do something better. For instance, a person may be at work and need a coach to help them achieve a certain outcome on a task. However, a mentor, is a person who is willing to take a personal interest in ensuring that the mentee reaches his/her goals. They stretch the person and train them in their area of expertise. Think succession. A boss taking someone under their wing to show them the in's-and-outs and *preparing* them in every aspect of the business.

Accountability partners are individuals who are willing to hold a person accountable for their actions. Accountability partners and mentors should be selected using wisdom. I also recommend that you have multiple mentors and multiple accountability partners.

Choosing a mentor

Remember, a mentor is a person that is willing to invest in you and pour knowledge and wisdom in you from their level of expertise. So, in this case you may have a professional mentor who will help you achieve your goals professionally. You may also have a mentor on a social level, educational level, or perhaps spiritual level. As you grow and develop, your need for different mentors will change over time. Having a good mentor is invaluable to our growth and advancement personally and otherwise. I suggest having between three and five mentors.

The Consequences of Choosing the Wrong Mentor

If you are trying to experience success in your personal life, career or business, it may be beneficial for you to find a mentor. Most of the time, a mentor can help guide you in the right direction as well as giving you the chance to learn from their mistakes. A mentor can give you advice that you might not have thought of, therefore leading to greater, more balanced decisions.

Choosing a mentor is important. It is even more important to choose the right mentor for you. Your mentor has to be someone with the right qualities, someone that will steer you in the right direction as well as someone you feel comfortable with and that you can work well with. The mentor you choose must have more than just the right qualities, but also the right level of expertise in order for it to be a successful partnership.

Your mentor should be ahead of you on the path you have chosen to take, whether that be a personal or business journey. Having someone who is at/on the same level of you is not going to work. Your mentor needs to be similar to you in the sense that they have similar goals and life values as well as wanting to share their advice with you without feeling threatened or disheartened by your success.

True, you could find someone that you greatly admire but that is not quite enough to make a good mentor. This is a two-way relationship street so your mentor should have the time and energy to invest in you as well as you in them. You both have to believe in each other for the partnership to work and be successful.

Another thing, honesty is key. If you don't have honest discussions about your goals, values, morals, etc., then you can't gain the best results possible. You will learn from the experience, mistakes and the years of wisdom that your mentor has endured, but it is important to remember that they will also learn from you. They may learn new techniques or ways to do things that they hadn't thought of. Again, it's a two-way relationship.

Finding the right mentor can mean a fast track on your goals and dreams, having the experience and wisdom of a mentor can be highly helpful.

The Value of a Good Mentor

Why is it that as we progress through our lives, we often get the message that we have something to prove? We believe that we have to be proficient at everything in order to be considered successful. This was my story. However, what is it about our ego that causes us to value who we are, based on what others think?

Sadly, in our society this mindset is very common. Even more concerning is that in the work place environment it is prevalent. So often the culture we work in is overly competitive and each person is looking to "get theirs". We believe we have to continually prove ourselves or do things on our own so we aren't considered incompetent. We fear that someone else will make us look bad or worse, take our position. Is it our ego? What are we afraid of? Why don›t we help each other?

I have never understood why people don't cooperate and work together more often. Doesn't it make sense that collectively, we can accomplish more? What if it was the norm, not the exception, that you were able to get help from the people you interact with every day? What if your co-workers were people that cared about your success as much as you do? What if they wanted you to succeed, and together you found ways to empower each other? What if this ideal was already a reality that many successful people tap into each and every day?

Suppose you knew that with this tool, your chances of success in your job and in your life would increase exponentially. If individuals took the time to invest in each other, coach up, and became truly concerned with ensuring that everyone moved ahead how better off would we be personally and professionally. A mentor is someone who could possibly serve in this capacity for you, and possibly give you the opportunity to pay it forward by mentoring someone else. That is why some successful people actively look for the perfect mentor. The Merriam-Webster dictionary defines a mentor as "a trusted counselor or guide." A mentor is actually someone who has more experience than you, and can share their knowledge with you. This individual has walked the walk you are just beginning and will make your journey more rewarding!

Entrepreneurs and executives seek the advice and support of mentors each and every day. For executives in certain areas, mentors are discovered through programs such as fellowships. It's part of how they do business, and how they advance their own careers and skill sets. People who make the most of working with their mentors can likely move up the ladder at a much quicker pace than those who venture out on their own. You may feel that you can handle things by yourself, and while that may be the truth, your career has the possibility to accelerate exponentially if you know the right people and understand what it takes to move forward. I have come to describe and know this as having a seat at the table.

A well chosen mentor has the capability to shorten the learning curve, introduce you to the right contacts, and create opportunities that you alone may not notice. Their value can be immeasurable, and can possibly take your career and your life to a higher level. The key to making the most out of your mentor relationship is to ensure you choose wisely. Usually, the best place to look for a mentor is right in front of you. Look around. Is there an individual whom you admire and respect? It could be someone who has always impressed you with their insight and perceptiveness, or maybe it is someone you don't know yet. Maybe it's a co-worker that took an idea and made an impact, or perhaps it's your boss. It could even be a retired individual who has lots of experience in a particular area.

When you start looking, you will be surprised at the number of people you know by whom you can be mentored.

The biggest key to choosing a mentor is to seek out the people you want to emulate. A good mentor can make a world of difference in how we succeed and progress in our careers, personal life, and spiritual life. They may offer you advice and guidance in getting ahead in the world, or give you encouragement when things are difficult. Most importantly, a good mentor will push you when you need to break through the fears that are holding you back. Many of these fears quite possibly can come from self-sabotaging behavior and procrastination. Here are a few guidelines and tips that can help you in selecting good mentors.

1. Think about your needs and what you would like your mentor to do for you. I caution you-it is important to have mentors that operate in their realm of expertise. Clear boundaries are important.
2. Think about and list possible mentors that fit that description.
3. Decide how you will approach the prospective mentor(s), when asking them to assist you.
4. Be patient, it may take some time before you find a person that you work well with that also meets your needs.

Like all worthwhile pursuits, finding a good mentor takes a little work and may involve stepping out of your comfort zone, but the benefits that you will gain will be worthwhile, and will make a huge difference in the future of your career.

What to Look For When Choosing a Mentor

As mentioned earlier, when you are taking on a goal, it is important that you find a mentor to guide you along the way. However, finding someone to mentor you is more than just picking someone at random, you need to be able to work well with the person and the person needs to be confident enough to ensure your success. When looking for a mentor, it is important to ask yourself the following questions:

Is the advice you want from the mentor general or specific? If specific, you'll want to find someone proficient in that area.

Do you want someone with similar values, goals and morals or someone that is completely the opposite? Some people may find it difficult to learn from someone who is similar to them. You need to find a mentor who suits you best, so be honest with each other about the kind of person you are.

Do you want your mentor to be your role model? As previously mentioned, your mentor should be someone who is on a higher level than you, therefore they can give you the advice you need to reach the place they are.

Does the person give advice that you consider to be good? Try asking this person for advice first before you decide to ask them to be your mentor. You don't want to get a mentor whose advice you don't think is worth your time. Not everyone can be a good mentor, no matter how successful they are.

What can you give this person in return? Sometimes it is necessary to be able to give your mentor something that keeps the relationship sweet, whether this is advice, feedback or just plain gratitude. Make sure that you express appreciation to your mentor; remember they are taking time out of their day to help you so be prompt, engaging and honest.

Do you need more than one mentor? Some people will require more than one mentor, especially if they have aspirations that one mentor cannot give advice on. For example, if you have a business aspiration you may need one mentor, and for personal aspirations you may see another.

Finally, have you checked whether this person actually wants to be your mentor? Remember they are taking time out of their day and giving you advice (most likely for free). Not everyone wants the commitment.

Choosing a good mentor takes time, so don't be disheartened if you don't find someone immediately. Look at several mentors and chances are, you'll find someone that's perfect for you.

Reflective Pause

Do you have mentors? If yes, how did you select them? Did you use a particular criterion? If no, after reading this chapter do you see the value of how mentors can aide you in achieving your professional, personal, and spiritual goals to name a few? Have you established clear goals and expectations?

What are the Benefits of Accountability Partners?

We are not meant to do everything on our own, especially when it comes to business. If you can find someone to hold you accountable for your lofty goals, you can achieve those targets much more quickly.

To get the most out of your relationship, consider the following:

- How your accountability partner measures and reports your progress.
- How your accountability partner reacts when you go off-track.

- How much ownership you assume for your actions.
- The way in which your company utilizes accountability will determine how you implement your strategy and achieve your goals. Having an accountability partner will affect every goal, task, and action, no matter how big or small.

The benefits that you can reap from your relationship with an accountability partner include:

Your performance will improve: When people know they are being held accountable by others for their actions, they will work harder.

You receive honest feedback: Just as you are committed to your goals, your accountability partner must be committed to giving you honest feedback, both positive and about areas where you need growth.

Having an accountability partner can keep you on track and improve your productivity. With this structure, it is unlikely you would become distracted from your goals. To avoid any feelings of being overwhelmed, an accountability partner can help you break down your goals into actionable and attainable steps.

You will be able to create deadlines: Your accountability partner will help you in reaching your goals by setting fixed and public deadlines.

You stay grounded: Accountability enables you to reinforce your goals regularly. It prevents you from becoming too optimistic and allows you to keep your feet on the ground, even when day-to-day tasks can seem mundane. Your partner helps you stay mindful of the present so that you can achieve your short-term goals.

You will keep problems or challenges in perspective: If you don't address small problems right away, they can quickly grow into bigger issues. There may be times when you inadvertently overlook concerns that need to be addressed. An accountability partner will provide you with a second pair of eyes, therefore helping you recognize concerns or challenges that you might not be able to see.

Nuts and Bolts of the Accountability Partner Relationship

When you find yourself an accountability partner, you are essentially agreeing to hold each other accountable for the other's actions. You need to agree to speak on a regular basis, as this is essential for maintaining motivation to reach your goals.

It would be ideal for you to check in with your accountability partner at least once a week. Therefore, your conversations are more frequent, and you'll be able to reach your goals much quicker. During the conversations, you should be updating your partner on how you are proceeding with goals, as well as setting new goals for the future. It would be ideal for you both to take notes, especially if you have agreed to tick off a certain goal in a certain time period, that way you can really keep each other accountable.

Maybe every other week, meet up in person with your accountability partner so you can have a longer discussion about your goals. This can also help to keep you motivated and allows you both time to give each other a perspective. For example, if you are finding a particular goal difficult to achieve, your accountability partner may have some ideas that can help you.

Accountability partners are similar to mentors, with a few significant differences. Your mentor is an experienced and trusted advisor who can teach you from their knowledge and experiences in a specified area of expertise.

Your relationship with a mentor is typically hierarchical, but an accountability partner will tend to be more relaxed and is more peer-to-peer.

One modern-day example is Oprah Winfrey stating that Maya Angelou (poet and author) was her mentor. Winfrey described Angelou as being "...there for me always, guiding me through some of the most important years of my life." Winfrey has also spoken of her accountability partners for her personal life, her buddies at Weight Watchers who help her to meet her weight loss goals.

While both relationships benefit Oprah's personal and professional growth, they fill different roles.

Choosing Accountability Partners

When it comes to choosing accountability partners the process can be tricky. Accountability partners are individuals you can be vulnerable with. These are people you can trust with some of your deepest feelings. Accountability partners do not necessarily have to be friends or family. However, if you select an accountability partner and they happen to be a friend or family member, understand it is important that you have very clear boundaries. Understanding boundaries are crucial when it involves both mentors and accountability partners. Here are a few things to think about when choosing an accountability partner.

- What is the nature of the relationship?
- Do you have a clear understanding of confidentiality?
- What are you agreeing to be held accountable for?
- How will they hold you accountable?
- How will they offer you feedback?
- What is your responsibility in receiving and responding to feedback?

Accountability partners are not *yes* people. They are individuals that will help you process your thoughts, feelings, and actions. I will admit, sometimes I can think I handled a situation the right way. However, after discussing how I handled the situation with my accountability partner, I realized I still had room for improvement. Even though, from my viewpoint, I felt as if I handled the situation correctly, my accountability partner was able to give me a different perspective.

For example, if one of my challenges is to deal with patience, I may have an accountability partner who will hold me accountable regarding that particular challenge. This person will tell me if I am right, wrong, or indifferent in how I handled a situation and is willing to help me process this area of my life.

I suggest having a minimum of three accountability partners; and not to exceed five. Remember this involves you being very transparent with these individuals. Keep this in mind: keeping this circle of trusted individuals small is highly recommended. Understand, accountability partners are not therapists. If you have deeper challenges that require a professional, please seek the help of a licensed professional.

Questions to Ask a Potential Accountability Partner

When you are trying to find someone to be your accountability partner, it is important to have an open and honest conversation about what you both expect from each other. The more upfront and honest you are, the easier your partnership will be. It is also important to speak about your goals and the challenges you have faced when trying to achieve these goals in the past, as your accountability partner may have some new ideas to put forward to help you achieve your goals. Therefore, they also have a better knowledge of their task in the future and what challenges you may face. The following are some questions that you might ask a potential accountability partner:

- What are some of your most successful motivators?

- What works to keep you focused when you set a goal, and what challenges have you faced in the past that you have struggled to overcome?

- Is there anything I should know that might create challenges for me as your partner in the future?

- Is there anything you can think of that will really help our partnership to succeed?

Reflective Pause

Do you have accountability partners? If yes, how did you select them? If no, after reading this chapter do you see the value of having accountability partners? Do you see how they can aid you in achieving your professional, personal, and spiritual goals, to name a few? If you have accountability partners, how effective have they been? Do you need different accountability partners? Have you established clear goals and expectations?

CHAPTER 15

FILLING MY CUP

I hope you are still with me and have learned a few helpful things along the way. For this next section let's talk a little more about what fills your cup. Meaning, employing the definition of self- which states what is needed to effectively fill your cup in your most needful space. The first thing you need to know is that it is your sole responsibility to ensure you are not operating from a place a depletion. So often we depend on others to pour into us when it is us who needs to learn how to be poured into and what that looks like for us. The problem many people face and frankly get very frustrated with, is not understanding what they need to fill their cup. Again, the better you know your story and can identify what depletes you, the more aware you will become of what frees you and fills your cup.

Hypoxia! The Importance of Filling your cup first

Have you ever taken a ride on an airplane? If you have ever taken the opportunity to listen to the stewardess go over the safety instructions before take-off, you may have heard them give the following information: if the cabin were to lose pressure a mask will suspend from overhead. They continue to say, oxygen will flow from the mask, and to ensure you put your mask on first before assisting someone else. The reason they give these instructions is due to a word called hypoxia, which simply means deprivation from oxygen. See, if you lose oxygen trying to help someone else and you pass out, the chances are that not only the person you are trying to help may not survive, but it is almost certain that you will not survive, as the body can only go so long without adequate oxygen. Now, let's look at this another way, if you can imagine your cup to be your personal supply of energy. If you don't look after yourself, your energy levels will go down, meaning you are risking not being able to contribute to your job, family, friends and even yourself. Think about it, is your cup full? Are you looking after yourself, and do you feel happy?

Your job is to make sure that your cup of energy is full, so that you can be there for other people who might not have a full cup of energy. Despite this, having a depleted energy level means that you aren't looking after yourself properly.

When thinking about your cup of energy, and what it takes to fill it, remember that your focus is to enjoy life and get the most out of it. This means enjoying your experiences and the people that you are with, which makes life more fun in the long run. Doing all this while getting everything done that 'must be done' is an important goal in life. This will promote a motivated, productive lifestyle, but also a fun one.

When I speak to people about self-care the top two responses as to why people explain they don't take time for themselves are:

1. don't have time.
2. didn't want to appear as if I was being selfish.

Many people think taking time for themselves is selfish. However, I disagree! Most people sacrifice themselves and their well-being for their job, their friends, or their family, but I think time should definitely be taken to slow down and focus on ourselves once in a while. It's important to set boundaries for dividing your time, otherwise there's none left for yourself.

It is a well-known fact that people are much more mentally and physically strong when they take time for themselves.

You can be the best version of yourself when you look after yourself, whether mentally, spiritually, physically or emotionally. If you take time to feel calm, relaxed, and pampered, you're more likely to be of better help to your family and friends, as you will have the energy to devote to the people you love. Therefore, you are better able to appreciate your life and the people in it.

It is heart-breaking to see how people can live life without truly living life. I say this from a personal space. I have lived at least half of my life expectancy, and not too long ago, I changed my mentality to truly live and embrace life. I finally said to myself, I don't need another degree, another accolade, or a big contract, in order to experience joy. No, I need to be present, and I needed to give myself permission to not have to be the best.

Think about it, would you want your friend, partner or parent feeling as though they were worn out dealing with your issues without taking care and time for themselves? No, of course you wouldn't. So why do we feel guilty for taking the time we need when a parent, partner, or friend needs us? We all need to fill our cup of energy before we get too depleted that we are worn out and cannot do the things we love with the people we love.

Filling Your Own Cup

When you are worn out and depleted of energy, it is hard to function at all, within your job or within your friendships.

This is why taking care of yourself has become so important in today's society.

Whether you are a person who already takes the time for yourself or if you are the person that needs to, hopefully this book can help you learn to care for yourself before you care for others. My mother always said that the only person you go to bed with every single night of your life is yourself, so pay attention to this! If you aren't caring for yourself, how can you care for others?

Therefore, filling your own cup of energy before anyone else's is so important so you are able to be the best version of yourself for you and everyone around you. If you really look after yourself and understand your needs, you'll then be able to be there for the other people in your life.

I'm definitely one of those people that put others before myself; however, sometimes your needs have to be a priority, you have to be able to feel energized and emotionally stable in order to better serve your friends and family.

What Depletes you?

There have been times in everyone's life where they are worn out and have absolutely no energy. In everyday life, there is always something that requires all or most of your energy and time. Some are unexpected, like losing a loved one, celebratory preparations or even a busy week at work.

This is when you must practice self-care the most, you need to make sure that you have enough energy to get through the day. Trust me when I say, I have tried to do it all, and when I did, it surely came at a cost. Have you ever been dog tired, but not able to sleep? Have you ever had so much on your mind that you can't remember what you were thinking about? Or have you laid down for an hour just to get back up to start your day all over again? Lastly, have you ever felt like a hamster on the wheel doing the same thing over and over again? If so, like me, I believe it's time to make some significant changes.

No Excuses - Make the Time Necessary

I cannot count how many times people have told me "there isn't enough time in the day." In fact, I say this quite regularly. Of course, everyone is busy and could use a few more minutes sleep or a few more minutes here and there. But how many times a day do you take the time to just relax and take a moment to yourself?

If you don't feel like this is something you do, you definitely need to make more time for yourself. You need to practice self-care. Self-care is so important to rejuvenating our energy resources and sometimes it can give us a fresh perspective. I find that if I take two minutes to walk outside and breathe some fresh air after being inside all day, I come back to my computer with a fresh new idea or perspective.

Whether you are a mother, you work full-time or you are retired, everyone deserves time to themselves. Self-care is important. Whether you spend two minutes in the fresh air like I do, or an hour in the bath with a candle and a good book, make sure you take that time for yourself. Avoiding doing this could mean you burn-out and stop being there for the people you love or avoid doing the activities that you love doing. Take the time for yourself.

Think about it, do you need to do a better job of setting aside a time just for yourself? Although you might feel slightly selfish at first, this self-care time that you are intentionally setting aside could mean you feel fresh and replenished and can help your friend solve their issue. Of course, it will always seem as though there are more pressing things that need to be done but self-care puts you on the motivational path to getting these things done.

While Driving

I spend a great deal of my driving time as my *me* time. I used to get in the car, blast the music and sort of rock out. Being honest, I still do that from time to time. However, as I am getting older, quiet time to myself is more valuable. I spend a good amount of time in silence, to really gather my thoughts, feelings, or engage myself with how I want the day to go. Yes, I have to give myself a pep-talk every now and then.

Here are a few ideas that could help transform your daily drive into work that can be defined as 'you time'.

- **Listen to Something that will feeds you**

For me, a good amount of time I typically YouTube one of my favorite motivational speakers, teachers, or preachers. I try to listen to things that will feed me. Have you ever had a book you wanted to read, but you may say to yourself, I just don't have the quiet time I would like in order to really get into the book? If that is the case, think about an audio book. I find them relaxing and they are good for when you don't have the time to sit down and read a paperback. From my experience, most audio books are around 20 hours long so it would only take you a few weeks of driving to work before you finish it. You can find audio books anywhere on the Internet and they aren't expensive to buy, yet this is a great way of relaxing and spending your time doing something that is just as rewarding as reading the paperback book.

Another option is to create an all-time old-school playlist. For me, I am a Michael Jackson and Stevie Wonder fan, so I will go through and listen to an 80's or 90's playlist. Again, finding balance is key. Somedays you may want an audio book, another day a motivational message or prayer, while other times good music may be the game changer regarding elevating your mood.

Make the Adjustment to get up Earlier

This may not be for everyone as for me I'm not the best morning person, but I have to agree that this is one way to 'self-care'. Getting up and cracking on with your work or chores, or whatever it may be feels good. Having a productive start to a day where you get up early and get everything done can have a big impact in your life

Even just getting up 30 minutes earlier can have a huge impact. What may work for you is simply sitting with a coffee in the morning reading your book or taking the time to connect with a loved one. You could spend this time exercising. Go outside for a walk to feel refreshed or take part in online yoga. All of this is part of self-care. I'll share this example. While on a trip to Tennessee, I stayed with my cousin. Now he is an earlier riser. His morning routine is to get up around 5am and go for a stroll in the neighborhood. He uses this time to relax and at times ease his mind so that he can enter a creative space. Now when, I came to visit, he said, cousin we can wake up about 5am. Of, course I stopped him before he could finish the sentence. Saying, "No sir". However, after suffering a health challenge due to contracting the Corona Virus, which led to a 3-day hospital stay in an ICU unit, I was very weak and extremely fatigued so much so that walking up a flight of stairs was challenging. However, I said to myself, if I want to get my wind back, there are some changes I have to make. One of those changes, was to get up an hour early and do as my cousin did, walk which led to jogging, and eventually a combination of the two. What I gained, from these morning walks was definitely more clarity, structure, and purpose. One of which, this book in itself was a byproduct of.

Identifying What Fills Your Cup

Take the time to think about what fills your cup. Is it meditating, reading, or exercising? Take the time, whether it is every day or just once a week to really focus on doing something you love. This is self-care. You are taking the time to spend some time by yourself, doing something you love, that will energize and refresh you. If you don't know what you love to do, go out and try things! You never know, you might have fun trying.

Where are you mentally, emotionally, physically and spiritually when your cup needs to be filled?

The world is going through trying, confusing and maybe anxiety provoking times with the Covid-19 pandemic. This has resulted in decreased structure, decreased social interaction, increased uncertainty, and many difficult emotions and thoughts for all. Stressors will reduce our capacity for coping and managing during challenging times. Take note, it is not only during times like these that we need to be aware of personal care and building our resilience. It is imperative that we are intentional and consistent in applying self-care techniques at all times. We need to be proactive to life and not reactive.

Life always has seasons of trial and struggle, pressure and tension; however, we are able to cope, overcome and walk victoriously. Remember that these simple yet essential tips will not implement themselves, you need to take personal responsibility and apply them on a regular basis in order to benefit. They will not result in instant gratification (some may) but will lead to healthier, long lasting, positive outcomes. Fill your personal self-care cup and increase your levels of resilience in order to remain at optimal levels of functioning. We need to implement these coping skills in order to deal with stress, problems, challenges and difficult seasons of life.

Personal self-care covers a range of different areas in our lives- physical, psychological (emotional and mental) and most importantly, spiritual. We will go over a series of write ups, looking at how to care for oneself. Become more conscious and aware of how you care for yourself holistically. Remember that body, soul, and spirit all need to be fed, cared for and focused on.

WHY have you selected those people and self-care methods to help fill your cup?

So, this one seems like a bit of a no-brainer. Clearly, spending time with people with whom you can connect, who help you feel understood, and who make you a better person, is good for you. Here are some tips and ideas that I've been trying to do in order to make sure I'm spending time with those that fill my cup.

Honestly, the first step is figuring out who is actually a cup-filler in your life. This might seem obvious—like your friends wouldn't be your friends if they weren't good for you. But take a little bit of time to truly assess how you feel when you are around them—do you feel happy, supported, challenged, cared for, and like you're becoming a better person due to the time you spend with them? Or is it opposite. Clearly, all friendships have their ups and downs, so I'm not saying that the friend who is currently going through a very difficult time and is therefore needy, isn't someone who fills your cup—especially if this is a friend who has also seen you through thick and thin. But to quote a friend of mine, you may need to "trim the fat" in order to make time to enjoy the true cup-fillers.

When you think of one of these friends and miss them or wish you could spend time with them (even if right now, schedules don't permit) ...let them know. All too often we forget to let those we care about know when we are thinking about them and the important role they play in our lives. By letting them know, it can go a long way to deepening the friendship.

Instead of saying, "we should get together again soon", go ahead and propose a date! If I'm not careful, I can become a procrastinator with not getting together. My schedule, their schedule, family schedules. So next time, one of your cup-filling friends (or someone you think could become a cup-filler,) says "let's get together soon", set the date right then and there and ensure you stick to it!

Speaking of one-on-one time...figure out what works with your friendships in regard to one-on-one versus groupings. Some friendships blossom with one-on-one time, others seem to work themselves into small groups that just make the perfect combo. I'm not saying you won't mix it up every now and then (and you know hang out with one of the "group friends" one-on-one or visa versa), but I think it's totally beneficial to acknowledge what works—and then plan time together accordingly.

Quick questionnaire guide

- **Where** - Are you at this time in your life that you need to be filled? (knowing where you are in life is important)
- **Who** - Fills your cup? Knowing who feels your cup is essential to knowing who is responsible for feeling your cup.
- **Why** - Did you choose these people?
- **How** - How do they feel your cup?

- **What** - What is needed to fulfill your cup?
- **When** - At what point do you need your cup to be refilled? What level do you not operate so well? Don't let your cup get below a certain point. Do not wait until you are depleted.

As this chapter comes to a close, one of the most important aspects to effective self-care is understanding that self-care is not static, but progressive. As we grow, we change, and we all encounter some of the curve balls that life throws at us. Where you are in life absolutely matters and makes a difference as to what is needed to fill your cup. In the next section we will discuss additional aspects to selfcare.

Reflective Pause

What have you learned in this chapter? Do you have good self-care practices? Do you practice enough self-care? Have you identified things or people who fill your cup and those who drain your cup?

CHAPTER 16

THE FOUR R'S

In a presentation I gave on self-care, I used four words as the premise to what I believe better aids in the self-care process.

The first R is *retreat*.

When I first thought of the word retreat, I thought of it negatively. Most often, I would hear the word retreat, and associate it as a form of weakness, such as one retreating in battle. However, I would offer the advice that there is great benefit in a retreat, which simplistically is defined as 'to withdraw from or step away from'. Think of it in this way.

Many times, when we are working hard on a project or task, we become frustrated due to either the loss of focus or the intense amount of energy we give to it. Historically, we have been taught to take a step back, leave it alone for a while, and then re-engage, which offers us time to recalibrate and engage with a fresh perspective. We not only employ this tactic to projects, but also to intense debates and arguments.

To retreat can be such a powerful asset in our toolbox if we only recognize how to use it properly. If you are anything like me, I would often push the envelope to get things done. On occasion, I have had to go back and redo things, due to silly mistakes I have made, just for the sake of getting things finished. I recall putting together a cabinet from Ikea. The directions were not the best, but I was determined to get the cabinet put together.

During the course of putting it together, I became frustrated. When I completed the project, I realized that I had put some of the cabinet pieces together backwards. My inability to walk away from it resulted in my having to completely disassemble the cabinet and start all over again. Now, I am a pretty handy person, however, no matter how skilled or handy a person may be, mistakes are bound to happen when you add in the element of frustration.

As it pertains to timing, retreating sometimes isn't effective because we retreat too late. To say it in another way, we fail to step back to gain better perspective, and allow ourselves the time needed to breathe before reengaging.

Companies send people on retreats from work, which actually are not retreats, but more or less additional trainings. I have worked in Corporate America, and have been on many retreats, and most of them as I explained, were training sessions at hotels. While I was away from work, I literally substituted work for additional work.

These were not retreats which allowed me the time to get away and withdraw. For the sake of self-care, a retreat should be seen as a means to simply decompress. This is not merely a vacation, spa day, or a pamper day.

These elements could very well be part of a retreat, but do not encompass the significance and goal of a retreat's purpose. Guided retreats are helpful and insightful because they help navigate the journey to wholeness.

Guided retreats with a focus on calm and stillness that allow time for focus, clarity and rejuvenation are extremely important and vital to our overall health. Retreats that are stand-alone vacations are helpful and needed also, but often do not give us the necessary tools we need for sustainable self-care.

Retreats are more than just for work. There are personal retreats, couple retreats, leadership retreats, and spiritual retreats to name a few. For *personal* retreats, a person may need something that is for them alone. *Couples* retreats are good for couples who are interested in recalibrating their marriage, commitment, or bond with one another.

Couple retreats are fantastic for those seeking to move together in partnership with one another whilst gaining clarity and focus. *Leadership* retreats are held near and dear to my heart, and for this reason, my consulting company really focuses on hosting customized retreats for leaders. Leaders are often thrust into decision-making roles on a daily basis.

Many leaders have a hard time shutting their brains off. I have seen many leaders crumble due to heavy loads and being overworked. Once you become a leader, you have a mantle of responsibility to ensure everything runs smoothly. This comes with a lot of pressure and sometimes anxiety. Having a guided retreat which helps us to center ourselves and become relaxed, while also gaining new perspective, is priceless.

When I was a private school teacher, the faculty started each year with a staff retreat. During one particular off-campus retreat, we had an excellent facilitator who engaged everyone. I recall the staff sitting in a circle and engaging one with another.

There was not a lot of "to do" stuff, but the retreat offered us time to get away to reflect, refresh and regroup. The retreat was so impactful, and it was probably one of my best years teaching high school.

Reflect

The second R stands for reflect. A major part of a retreat should encompass a time of reflection. During this portion, participants can often reflect on what has worked well and what hasn't. For instance, if we were thinking of a marriage retreat, a couple could ask themselves "what has worked well in our marriage and what areas need adjustment?"

For individuals on a personal or self-retreat they may reflect on something that deals with them individually, be it personal or professional. Often, this is the part we fail at most. Allowing ourselves the proper time without interruptions and distractions to truly reflect. Think from the perspective of relationships for a moment. A person has been in a committed relationship for a particular amount of time. The relationship then suffers a breakup, and person A quickly jumps into another relationship.

In this scenario, a time period to figure out and reflect on the positives and negatives of what person A contributed to the relationship, be it good, bad, or indifferent could better assist them in having a healthier relationship down the road. However, failure to truly reflect on what took place in the relationship will often manifest in the new relationship. The person may seek the exact opposite of his or her previous relationship or end up in the exact same situation they were in beforehand.

When we genuinely reflect, it allows us to take a personal inventory on how our actions have contributed to any given outcome. This is pivotal to self-care as it allows us to be vulnerable, but also it raises our awareness to areas that we may have overlooked and possibly never thought of. In terms of profession, which is not much different than personal relationships, reflecting can offer insight into how we relate to others. I will be the first to say that I have worked for some horrible bosses. However, I have also worked for a few awesome ones. One that I will speak of in this book, was my Sergeant First Class in the United States Army. I learned a great deal from him as a firm, consistent and fair leader, and his strength as a leader has also influenced my leadership style. Many of the soldiers under his command not only respected him, but also looked up to him. When I evaluated myself during my time of reflection, I asked myself very transparent questions. Questions such as "How do I see myself? Am I being true to myself? Am I leading my team or people in a way that I can be proud of? What adjustments can I make to be a better person and a better leader? What changes need to be made to the way I process, due to the changes of culture and time?"

From the perspective of a spiritual retreat and reflecting on my relationship with a higher power, this is applicable across various faith traditions. In fact, after a training I had in the hospital, one of my Buddhist colleagues offered to help me have some quiet time and center myself, so I could become more mindful and reflective. Due to her willingness, it gave me an experience that I found to be priceless.

For the first time, I was able to finally center myself. This was major, given my personality to go, go, go. Yes, it was awkward, but after some time I was able to embrace the quiet space.

Again, when we pause, and we are able to engage ourselves in a transparent and mindful manner, and truly reflect. Reflection can very well lead to a refreshing, renewing, and freeing experience, which leads to the path of becoming whole, healed and free from past hurt, trauma, and pain. During the reflective stage, you do not have to have the answers or solutions to fix anything. During this stage you are simply asking yourself questions, both easy, difficult, and everything in between.

Replenish

After we are able to get away from the busyness, withdrawing from it all and have the time to reflect, we have a need to be refreshed for this stage as we have to think about what refreshes or replenishes us. This will differ for each person based on their situation.

There are times we are challenged with enjoying this stage, because we have not yet retreated. I hope you noticed by now, retreating and reflecting encompasses mental, emotional, and spiritual self-care. While the refreshing stage also encompasses emotional self-care, it closely focuses on the physical aspect.

What replenishes me includes a good workout followed by the spa (sauna, steam room, hot tub, pool or plunge pool), engaging in good conversation, playing games (football, basketball, chess, cards, dominoes) and doing a host of activities that bring me joy.

While I am not that great at golf, I love the competitiveness in playing the game or any game that I can enjoy the time and company of others. I enjoy many of the same things that a great deal of people love to do on a vacation as long as it does not become too busy and grants me sufficient "me time". The really cool thing about the refreshing stage is that it entails whatever rejuvenates us and brings us life.

Replenish: Looking After Your Body, Soul and Spirit

Every machine, like a motor vehicle or a washing machine, suffers wear and tear if it is not cared for properly with regular servicing. Appropriate maintenance is vital for machines. The same can be said for our own bodies. Many of us are tougher on ourselves than on our cars. We become very frustrated at any suggestion we might need to rest or slow down for any reason.

Now I know people who can function off of a good power nap, and there is nothing wrong with that. However, power naps cannot supplement the value of a good night's rest. In other words, it's like pushing yourself all the time and only using a quick sleep or a tough workout at the gym to unwind. It does the job, but it is not good for the long-term health of your battery. You need a slow trickle charge on regular occasions as well to rid your body of adrenaline overdoses and help you to fully relax. [28]

For this reason, if we are to have a meaningful life, it is important to understand the need for consistent emotional and spiritual replenishment.

Replenishment: a Whole of Life Approach

When you really take the time to think about it, self-care is your personal investment in you. Self-care is taking the time to learn how to replenish yourself in every facet. Hopefully, by now the reoccurring message is pushing you toward wanting to have meaningful self-care strategies to position yourself toward being the healthiest version of you.

We need to evaluate how much we invest in ourselves, mainly in three significant areas:

Body – our physical being and health

Soul – mind (thinking), emotions (feeling)

Spirit – core, heart or inner-self.

We encounter most of our significant problems when we operate from a place of depletion. As we grow and mature and experience life, different challenges occur that affect us differently. What may have affected you in your earlier years may not affect you now. Subsequently, what affects you now may not have affected you in your earlier years. As we age, we may not respond the same to the common stressors of life. For some, getting older is a glorious thing, while others struggle with aging. Stressors ease for some and become greater for others. Paying attention to what works to fill each area is important to your overall effectiveness of self-care.

Restore

The last of the four R's is the word *restore*. In the restoration stage, which I also call regrouping, one is able to put everything together. With our new found self-awareness and mindfulness, our clarity and ability to refocus, and after being refreshed with things that fill us, it is now time to put our new strategies and resources together.

As a leader you may decide you need help. You may return from your retreat to engage your staff in a new way and solicit different ideas and gain feedback. Whatever and however this looks for you depends on you and what you believe to be the best course of action. When we are able to make decisions from a healthy space, solicit guidance and feedback, and engage a team from that healthier space, we are working towards great things.

Note, in this stage, we should not be afraid to use our resources. If we lack the resources needed to put such a plan together, I again strongly urge you to build relationships with individuals who will be of the greatest value. This stage, is equally important as any other, as it serves as the action stage. Before you put an action plan in place, you should have individuals who are willing to support you. These people **should also feel free to be very honest with you, ensuring you have dotted your I's and crossed your T's.**

How to Restore Yourself

Disconnect to reconnect yourself. One valuable thing you can do is to take a step back. Unplug from being so accessible. Today, we are more accessible than ever before. We allow cellphones and technological accessibility to dictate our lives. If it is not work, its social media, if not social media, it's checking emails or staying up to speed on the newest and greatest new fad. Again, disconnecting yourself even for a set amount of time can be significant to your mood and total wellbeing. When we can successfully disconnect, it gives us the fortitude to move forward, allowing ourselves to be fully immersed in relaxing without distractions or outside influences but only check them sporadically and only return calls for things that truly need immediate action.

Reassess your life. You may be feeling stressed because you realize you are not meeting your own needs or expectations. Look at the things that make you unhappy in your life and try to find ways to improve those areas. Remember, this is an action stage. Changes could be as small as blocking off 10 minutes a day to sit and meditate or as large as changing careers or scenery, perhaps relocating. Take the steps you feel will best help you restore your energy and regain control in your life.

Implement various relaxation strategies. There are all kinds of things you can do to help restore yourself. You may wish to take up a new hobby, read more, or spend more time in social situations. Not all tips work for everyone, so choose the action tips that fit into your lifestyle and what is feasible for you.

Tips

If you continue to have extreme stress after attempting several rejuvenation techniques you may wish to consult your physician or other professionals.

Warnings

Do not ignore the stress and exhaustion you feel. This can have mental, emotional, and physical repercussions. Address negativity and stress as soon as possible and deal with them in an appropriate manner.

Reflective Pause

This was a very rich section. What areas of each of the four R's spoke to you? Have you ever truly been on a retreat or have many of your retreats been trainings? Have you experienced retreat, reflection, refreshing, and restoration separately? How about together?? If not, what would this look like for you? What did you find helpful in this section?

CHAPTER 17

SELF-CARE PURPOSE

In my experience I have personally wrestled with purpose. When an individual has no ideal goal or loses sight of what their purpose is, it can lead to depression, doubt, and as we spoke about earlier in the book undue or unbeknown stress. Now, this is not a book on purpose, that one will come later.

However, let me briefly discuss how self-care and purpose is related.

When a person feels that they don't have purpose or find themselves questioning their purpose, it can lead to depression. Take for instance a person who has worked as an engineer for most of their life.

They love the technical part of using their brain but feel unfulfilled. I have met many people who associate their career with their purpose. I have been one of them. My passion is teaching no matter what it is, I love teaching. I love to help people, and love to see when people progress.

Now, when the educational system changed, and I had to rebrand myself, it was extremely hard, because I attached my purpose to my career. I have had the opportunity to work in various fields and I have appreciated the experience, exposure, and knowledge that I have gained in each one of them.

While in transition during my education career, I was recruited to serve as a Director of Corporate Quality for a home care agency. I had the opportunity of working with one of the smartest people I know. I didn't have much experience in healthcare, but what I did have was pretty good analytical skills and I was very good at relating to people.

While working in this capacity, I learned so much about lean processes as my VP is a Six Sigma Master black belt (quality experts who are responsible for the strategic implementations within an organization.) Working under my VP was the most frustrating yet rewarding experience I had, as it stretched me and caused me to think differently.

Self-Care: Let's Start the Conversation

To think in the ways that I never would have thought of in times past. Many of the skills I learned helped me to approach life differently, be it personal or professional while I was progressing in my job, I felt as if something was missing. I felt as if I was not connecting with people on a level I had previously connected, such as when I was in the education field counseling, teaching and coaching football. I must admit I felt unhappy, even when things were going well. I thought that going on a vacation would solve the unhappy feelings I had, but it didn't. I started going out more with friends and spending more time with my family.

Yet, this did not stop the uneasiness I was experiencing. I had no clue after working for the homecare agency that I was actually grieving the loss of teaching and coaching.

Because I felt that teaching was my passion, I absolutely thought it was my purpose as well. In retrospect, I was working in a professional capacity excelling, but what I had recently lost was due to not really knowing who I was. Everything I was doing extracurricular wise was not easing this feeling of unease. Now when I look back from a self-care standpoint, I ask the question, what did my soul need at that time? It was none of the activities I was trying. What I needed was a space alone, a space to grieve, be it counseling, mentoring, coaching, or time to really engage, own, and sort out my feelings.

As I previously mentioned, when we put self-care in a box, suggesting that it is simply leisure activities, we lose the very essence in what self-care can be and what it really entails, which is to care for the total self.

Reflective Pause

There are many people who go through job loss, job transition, or let's just say life transitions, which cause them to question their purpose once the job loss or transition happens. We see this often with people who may have served in the military or those who have entered retirement. While my experience may not be yours exactly, what in this section speaks to you? Have you ever wrestled with understanding your purpose, knowing your purpose, or simply lost sight of your purpose?

CHAPTER 18

Additional Barriers to Self-Care

Negative Self-image

This is what we think but are scared to say. There isn't a great deal of people who knowingly admit to having a negative self-image. To view oneself negatively, for most people is a sign of weakness and vulnerability. I mentioned the word vulnerable before.

Vulnerability in most cases is highly associated with a weak point or weakness. However, I believe, vulnerability in itself also has a positive connotation, such as being vulnerable with your spouse and being vulnerable enough to allow your feelings and thoughts to be heard. Often, people cannot get the help they need to address problems and concerns due to their lack of vulnerability.

I have witnessed on many occasions people who have not been successful in life in certain arenas because they refuse to focus and talk about areas that they are deficient in. I have been guilty of this myself. Feeling like I had to have all the answers. When we put that amount of stress and pressure on ourselves, we are bound to make mistakes.

One thing I have learned is that some of my weaknesses are actually strengths. By being honest enough with myself and saying that I need help, and not viewing myself as inferior because of my need for help, actually works in my favor. I have had the opportunity to work in various industries and I learned a great deal from others who were smarter than me.

Many times, the wisdom imparted may not be for you at that moment but could be useful for you down the line. Through wisdom and life's experiences I've learned how false perceptions served as barriers to how I viewed myself. There were times I thought poorly of myself because others perceivably were more professionally or financially successful than I was. I allowed myself to create a negative self-image narrative where maybe I was not as smart as I thought I was. I experienced how easy it was to go down the rabbit hole of self-doubt. Maybe you have worked somewhere for years and you are the one to whom the company looks when issues need solving, but you are also the one who is often overlooked when it is time for promotion.

Whatever the case may be, many times we can slip into the mode of questioning ourselves and our abilities and become angry and bitter. Other manifestations of this can also be seen in overcompensating and by becoming overly competitive, which could be very toxic in our journey to becoming a healthier version of ourselves.

Toxins

Toxins come in various forms, from toxic people, relationships, practices, and behaviors. When we attempt to overcompensate, we risk overworking ourselves or venturing off into unhealthy behaviors which may further exacerbate our initial issue.

Hopefully, you can see by now how a negative self-image and self-doubt can have a negative impact on our ability to properly care for ourselves. While we are attempting to be something we are not, we create a façade, which after a while takes a toll on us mentally, physically, and emotionally. I had to realize that every good idea didn't mean I had to develop a new business plan and open a new business for it. Just because we may be gifted, doesn't mean we should venture into every opportunity. Balance is key.

CHAPTER 19

Resilience and Sustainability

Self-care plays an important role in our ability to have resilience. In the workplace or life in general, we will all encounter adversity. However, how we respond and bounce back from the adversities in life is essential. We can either not bounce back, bounce back, but we do not come back strong, or we can have resilience and bounce back stronger than before we encountered the adversity.

Resilience is something that takes time, as resilient individuals are people who are equipped to make use of their skills, resources and strengths to better cope and recover from challenges and adversity. In practicing self-care and self-awareness, this can aid a person in becoming more resilient.

Being resilient or becoming resilient is a process. Resilience often can refer to how well we handle pressure. There is a huge advantage in having the skill set and tools of resilience. So how do we develop these tools or skills? Resilience often lies in self-worth, confidence, positive attitudes, determination, and focus to name a few. The ability to be optimistic even in the face of adversity is important. Resilient people are not afraid to fail. In some cases, those who are resilient generally have positive attitudes and address pressure in a more efficient manner. As I mentioned in a previous chapter, the use of a self-pep-talk (Encouraging talk with yourself) is helpful. Society can sometimes give us a false understanding of what it means to fail. If we are not careful, we can begin to put aspects of who we say we are into buckets that really don't match who we know we are and what we know we can be. Have you ever self-sabotaged? Have you ever not operated at a level you thought you should have, and just counted it all as a failure? Well, if you haven't, I have. At times people can become their own worst enemy by what they tell themselves based off their own or others interpretation of who they are or should be. Think about the word *success*. At a glance, you may assume that a successful person like a Mark Cuban, Oprah Winfrey, or Warren Buffet has never failed at something. Well,

I beg to differ, many of the people we may hold in high regards have all failed at something. Yet they did not allow failure to determine who they are. What makes individuals like the aforementioned resilient, is the fact that when things do not work out, they continue to refine different ideas and methods, until it is successful. Successful individuals, survivors, and great entrepreneurs have this trait in common, they try. Michael Jordan said it best in his book *Driven Within*, "Everybody has talent, but ability takes hard work." "Never **say never, because limits, like fears, are often just an illusion.**" "**Always turn a negative situation into a positive situation.**" "**To learn to succeed, you must first learn to fail.**"[33]

So, one of the most important aspects to resilience is conquering the fears of can't and by having a certain level of drive and **confiden**ce.

Controlling Emotions

Another important part of resilience, aside from confidence and being willing to fail in order to learn, is emotional stability. To be even tempered, balanced and to approach things logically. I know, easier said than done, especially when emotions run high. Yet, I appeal to you that regulating your emotions is crucial to resilience as emotions in general can cause you to say or make decisions that have a significant impact. I have personally made some very poor life decisions based off emotions. Be it positive emotions or negative emotions. For example, have you ever been so happy and carefree that you made a decision based off being super happy? Only to think about it later, and you say to yourself, "oh crap, why did I do that"? or you may have been upset, and made a decision based off anger, and later found that your words or actions could have been better. The ability, to stop and breathe through tough situations and not become hasty is an essential part of resilience particularly in emergencies or crises.

Resilience bank account

Resilient people find ways to stay focused and connected. They also are aware on what is needed to get the job done or to achieve an expected outcome. Resilience again is a process. This process includes having balance. For example, let's consider a bank. A bank is a place where transactions are made. A bank can only survive based on deposits being more than withdrawals. The bank ensures it is not lending in the negative. This is the importance of proper self-care. When you have balance and have stored up a great deal of positivity, when stressful situations come, you have enough positivity, drive, and confidence in reserve to counteract depression and giving up. Again, think balance, think persistence.

Persistent individuals continue to find and try new ways to solve a problem until they find a solution for it, and this does not mean they always do it by themselves but rather they become more intentional and wiser as to how they use their energy and their resources (accountability partners and mentors).

Closing Remarks on Resilience

Psychology today suggests:

> *To fail is deeply human—as is the capacity to inspect, learn from and transcend failure. Ultimately, failures are the stumbling blocks on the proverbial path to success: The lessons they teach have implications for humility, maturity, and empathy. Furthermore, that doesn't mean, however, that one needs to pretend that it's pleasant to fail or ignore the frustration that arises when a goal falls out of reach (Think of the need for retreat). Instead, accepting the feelings that come with failure, being curious about them, and resisting the urge to judge oneself too harshly are all critical skills to practice (Think reflection). In addition to cultivating better emotional regulation, such skills may also provide lessons that will stop the failure from repeating itself in the future.* [34]

As we change and adapt to different aspects of life and the never-ending challenges life presents, we must pay attention to what is needed at the present time.

The year of 2020 was riddled with challenges. What many would consider normalcy, is now far from normal.

The global effects of the Covid-19 pandemic, deaths, social injustices, politics, and a world that has seemingly been turned upside down all pose different stressors for different people. From families spending an unprecedented amount of time together with periods of little to no activities. Schools being shut down, churches closed, jobs lost. No one could have predicted the catastrophic effects that took place in 2020.

Even the most resilient people were tested. How could anyone be resilient in such an unusual time? Your normal modes of self-care may not have been available. Normal resources, skills, and abilities may have been judged as ineffective. For this reason, it is important to understand just how important it is for one to be able to adapt to the current challenges of life.

Resilience, like self-care comes down to a person's willingness and ability to adapt.

Sustainability

Resilience is one thing; however, sustainability is another. We must not ignore the seemingly complex question: "How do we add sustainability to resilience?" I would argue that self-care is needed. Burnout is so prevalent as we have seen in previous chapters. Competition and demands for being leaner, better, brighter, more advanced are at an all-time high. For this reason, self-care must be practiced more often. In the previous chapter I explained the necessity of the four "R's," and you may be thinking, "I don't have time to go on a retreat." However, the four "R's" is a guide to how you can use these tools every day. For instance, whenever I have had a tough and draining day, I can implement the four "R's."

After a rough day or week, I can shut off my phone and get out of the house. In Las Vegas, I've gone to Red Rock Canyon, turned off my phone and spent time centering myself. During very intense times, I've either gone with or spoken to a member of my accountability circle who was able to help me address, name, and identify areas to focus on.

Once I have gotten away from the chatter and quieted myself and reflected, I would go to the gym and get a good work out in and then hit the steam room, sauna, and hot tub which serves as part of me filling up my cup. If it is on the weekend, I might play golf with friends.

After completing that process, I regroup, and reengage stake holders, be it family, staff, or those in my accountability circle. Lastly, I always try to carve out a weekend, at least every other month, for me to take time to create a sacred place to exercise self-care and what that looks like changes based on what my body tells me I need for that specific space in time. For example, if I live in the city and I am constantly around noise. At that time in my life, as I practice self-care, my 'self-care time' may include a place where I can find quietness and stillness.

While on the other hand, a person who primarily occupies a quiet space may seek out a place that revives them that includes an element of increased noise. Within the past few years, I've purchased a pop-up camper, and have been known to go camping by myself in order to have that deep reflection and alone time.

Other times, I have planned and gone on guys camping trips and outings in which we all implemented the four "R's" and golfed together over the weekend. As part of self-care for my marriage, I ensure my wife and I have adequate time, be it camping or otherwise, where we can also implement the four "R's." These simple but powerful tools can serve you well in every aspect of your life.

We must take the proper time to take care ourselves in every aspect of our being. My hope for everyone who has read this book is that you were able to get some helpful tools to implement in your life so you can not only function better, but live healthier, less stressful, and more fulfilling lives.

When we effectively take care of ourselves, giving ourselves the proper attention needed, we make life better for ourselves and for those around us. We become better informed decision makers, more pleasant to be around and even better communicators.

The task of being a leader in any capacity comes with a host of challenges; however, having the right tools for the job is key in being successful in completing the job.

Reflective Pause

After reading this chapter I hoped it encouraged you to tap into your inner strength. Now I am going to ask you to reflect on a time that you struggled with being resilient. What was affecting your ability to be resilient? Have you ever struggled with sustainability? If so, what were the determining factors? After reading this chapter, what sections can you pinpoint, that will help you in becoming more resilient? What will help you in your area of sustainability?

CONCLUDING THOUGHT

If you quit on the process, you are quitting on the result -Koyenikan

Hopefully, you have had the opportunity to engage this book in a transparent way. When we are able to engage our story and have necessary pauses, we can become more aware of how our story informs our behaviors, patterns, attitude, and mood. By having a better understanding of self, we stand a much better chance of identifying what we need in order to renew and restore ourselves through self-care. Self-care being defined as what is needed to effectively fill your cup in your most needful space. Understanding and practicing self-care may involve utilizing multiple components simultaneously in order to reach your desired outcome while on your journey.

Your journey at various stages will most certainly call for different aspects and methods of self-care. Life, in itself, is not static. Life is ever-changing. This showcases the importance of ensuring we utilize the tools needed most at any given time.

Reference List

1. U.S. National Library of Medicine. (n.d.). Retrieved from https://medlineplus.gov: https://medlineplus.gov/stress.html

2. Hoekstra, M., & Hankins, S. (2011). *The Ticket to East Street? The Financial Consequences of Winning the Lottery.* Retrieved from: https://papers.ssrn.com/sol3/papers.cfm?abstract_id=1134067

3. Gillman, S. (2019). *From Rags to Riches to Rags Again: 21 Lottery Winners who Lost Everything.* Retrieved from: www.thepennyhoarder.com

4. McNulty, C. (2016). *Just Can't Escape the Daily Grind.* Chicago Tribune, Chicago.
5. American College of Healthcare. (2019, May 30). Retrieved from ache.org: https://www.ache.org/about-ache/news-and-awards/news-releases/hospital-ceo-turnover
6. American College of Healthcare. (2019, May 30). Retrieved from ache.org: https://www.ache.org/about-ache/news-and-awards/news-releases/hospital-ceo-turnover
7. Fuller Institute, G.B. (2016). *https://www.pastoralcare-inc.com.* Retrieved from: https://www.pastoralcareinc.com/statistics/
8. Anxiety and Depression Association of America. (n.d.). Retrieved from https://adaa.org/about-adaa/press-room/facts-statistics
9. Anxiety and Depression Association of America. (n.d.). Retrieved from https://adaa.org/about-adaa/press-room/facts-statistics
10. Haertl, K., & Christiansen, C. (2011). *Coping Skills.* In C. Brown & V.C. Stoffel (Eds.), *Occupational Therapy in Mental Health: A Vision for Participation (p. 313-329).* F.A Davis Company, Philadelphia.
11. Merrian-Webster. (n.d.). *Merrian-Webster, Dictionary.* & Duhigg, C. (2012). *The Power of Habit: Why We Do*

What We Do in Life & Business. Random House Trade Paperbacks, New York.

12. Duhigg, C. (2012). *The Power of Habit: Why We Do What We Do in Life & Business*. Random House Trade Paperbacks, New York.

13. Duhigg, C. (2012). *The Power of Habit: Why We Do What We Do in Life & Business*. Random House Trade Paperbacks, New York.

14. John Maxwell. (n.d.).

15. Haertl, K., & Christiansen, C. (2011). *Coping Skills*. In C. Brown & V.C. Stoffel (Eds.), *Occupational Therapy in Mental Health: A Vision for Participation (p. 313-329)*. F.A Davis Company, Philadelphia.

16. North Carolina State University. (2019). Retrieved from Counseling Center: https://counseling.dasa.ncsu.edu/self-care/

17. North Carolina State University. (2019). Retrieved from Counseling Center: https://counseling.dasa.ncsu.edu/self-care/

18. Cloud, H., & Townsend, J. (1992). *When to Say Yes, When to Say No, to Take Control of Your Life*. Zondervan, Michigan.

19. Unknown. *The Raccoon Story*.

20. Bible. English Standard Version.

21. Bible. English Standard Version

22. Bible. English Standard Version
23. Bible. English Standard Version
24. Bible. English Standard Version
25. Bible. English Standard Version
26. Bible. English Standard Version
27. Bible. English Standard Version
28. Bible. English Standard Version
29. Bible. English Standard Version
30. Bible. English Standard Version
31. Bible. English Standard Version
32. Cloud, H., & Townsend, J. (1992). *When to Say Yes, When to Say No, to Take Control of Your Life.* Zondervan, Michigan.
33. Jordan, M. (2005). *Driven from Within.* Atria Books, New York.
34. Unknown. (2009). *Resilience.* Retrieved from: https://www.psychologytoday.com/us/basics/resilience